"The brilliance of this system is it is so simple, practical and applicable that you will actually do it! I believe the more people who learn The 5C Solution, the better the world will become."

—**Dr. Clint G. Rogers**, university researcher and author of *Ancient Secrets of a Master Healer*

"Every once in a while, someone comes up with a system that simplifies complex problems, and that is what Cindy has done with The 5C Solution. I think it's brilliant."

—**Jack Canfield**, co-author of *Chicken Soup for the Soul* series

"The minute you pick up this book and begin reading, it will captivate you. To say the story of Cindy is gripping and miraculous would be an understatement! From complete emotional and spiritual bankruptcy to writing an inspiring book to help others overcome is truly extraordinary. Her deep courage and determination will give you hope for your own journey.

Her message throughout the book is ... "All things are possible with God, hope and never giving up." The 5C Solution is easy to understand and apply to your own life's experiences. If you need personal, emotional, spiritual or professional courage, this is the book for you."

—**Anne Beiler**, motivational speaker, founder of Auntie Anne's Pretzels

"There are certain things in life you have to experience before you can teach others. When it comes to overcoming heartbreak and struggle, Cindy has been through the fire, and from that fire came her passion and credibility to help others transform their lives. All too often self-help books are encouraging but lack clarity and credibility. This book has both, and will inspire and teach readers how to move forward when life is complicated and confusing. *The 5C Solution* provides a powerful step-by-step tool to discover your unique answers."

—**Weldon Long**, author of *The Upside of Fear, Consistency Selling* and *The Power of Consistency*, a NYT & WSJ Bestseller

"The 5C Solution is a powerful guide to find your pathway to healing through self-acceptance and self-love. It is authentic, original, and realistic. Self-acceptance is knowing the truth about yourself and is a necessary first step towards self-improvement. Hence, the power of Cindy's 5C Solution is undeniable."

— **Dr. Lem Burnham,** PhD, assistant chair of Behavioral Science and Psychology; associate professor at Wilmington University; Philadelphia chapter vice president of the NFL Alumni Association

THE 5C SOLUTION

Discover Clarity & Confidence in Times of Change

CINDY CIPRIANI

Helical House

The 5C Solution: Discover Clarity & Confidence in Times of Change
Copyright © 2020 by Cindy Cipriani
All rights reserved.

This book contains a partial memoir. It reflects the author's present recollections of experiences over time. Names and characteristics have been changed, some events have been compressed, and some dialogue has been recreated. The examples containing clients or other individuals are compilations of similar stories and do not represent the disclosure of any confidential information.

The author of this book does not dispense medical or psychiatric advice, nor prescribe the use of any technique as a form of treatment for medical or psychiatric problems without the advice of a physician or therapist, either directly or indirectly. The intent of the author is only to offer information of a general nature to help you in your quest for emotional well-being. In the event you use any of the information in this book for yourself, the author and publisher assume no responsibility for your actions.

U.S. Trademark Reg No. 4,997,624: Clarity · Commitment · Challenges · Creation · Celebrate

ISBN: 978-1-7346221-0-2

Printed in the United States of America

Website: https://www.the5csolution.com

Cover and interior design by Constellation Book Services

To my Heavenly Father.
Thank you for using me as a
vessel for this message.

Contents

Introduction   1

My Story: From Chaos to Clarity   7

Quick Start: Gaining Control Is at Hand   21

Part I: The 5C Solution   29

    Chapter 1: Clarity   31

    Chapter 2: Commitment   73

    Chapter 3: Challenges   79

    Chapter 4: Creation   85

    Chapter 5: Celebrate!   91

Part II: Practical Application of the 5C's   97

    Chapter 6: The 5C Solution for Everyday Life   99

    Chapter 7: The 5C Solution in Business   109

    Chapter 8: The 5C Solution in Relationships   119

    Chapter 9: The 5C Solution after a Breakup or Loss 131

    Chapter 10: The 5C Solution for Teens   137

    Chapter 11: The 5C Solution for Blended Families   149

    Chapter 12: The 5C Solution for Planning Your Future   157

Conclusion   161

Acknowledgments   163

Resources   167

Introduction

Chances are you picked up this book because life has thrown you into a situation you never imagined or planned. You might be unhappy, unfulfilled, and depressed. Maybe your heart was broken, or your relationship or marriage is in trouble or ending. Perhaps someone you love has passed away or become seriously ill. Maybe you just lost your job, your business is struggling, or the bottom dropped out of the economy. Perhaps you were or are being emotionally, physically, or mentally abused.

All these circumstances can be highly emotional and leave you feeling lost, frustrated, and confused. Time can seem to stand still when your emotions are so raw that you can't think clearly. One question keeps repeating in your mind: "What am I supposed to do *now*?"

Do you feel figuring out what to do next would be easier if you had a clear and memorable tool to immediately find answers? That is what I wanted.

I personally experienced all the situations described above, and tried everything people suggested. I read stacks of self-help books, watched famous psychologists on television giving scraps of advice to people in situations like mine, and went to professionals hoping to discover what to do when I was feeling overwhelmed, puzzled, or depressed. Unfortunately, I didn't find answers. Either the books were too complicated, the television shows were too general or the professionals lacked answers and empathy. I then asked God to help me find a new way to help not only myself but anyone who was living in chaos and confusion.

When people hear my life story, they ask how I went from so much heartbreak and loss to the vibrant person I am today. I can honestly say it was because of The 5C Solution. After this simple five-step formula took me from the pit of despair to the joy of celebration, I started teaching it to others using my hand as a memory tool. I soon realized that it helped everyone who used it.

What are the 5C's? I won't keep you wondering. Put your hand out in front of you with your fingers outstretched. Each finger represents one of the 5C's: *Clarity* (pinky finger), *Commitment* (ring finger), *Challenges* (middle finger), *Creation* (pointer finger), and *Celebrate!* (thumbs up).

This is the tool that I used for years when I volunteered at mentoring programs. Then in 2009 my business, Clear Path by Cindy, was born to teach people how to go from chaos to clarity. My retreats, workshops, and individual sessions are based on The 5C Solution. Helping people find their best life after loss or change is my greatest joy.

Lives are quickly changed by using this tool. Yours can be too!

Let's do a quick survey of where you are now. Circle the Stressors in your life:

CATACLYSMIC EVENTS   FRUSTRATION

CHRONIC STRESSORS   PLEASING EVERYBODY

I HAVE TO BE PERFECT   COMPARING TO OTHERS

I'M NOT GOOD ENOUGH   FINANCIAL PROBLEMS

CONFLICT

FEAR OF FAILURE

LIMITING BELIEFS

SOURCES OF STRESS

ILLNESS

DEATH OF A LOVED ONE

ABUSE   HASSLES

BEING A CAREGIVER   RELATIONSHIP PROBLEMS

MOVING HOUSE   PAST TRAUMAS & DRAMAS

DIVORCE   OCCUPATION BURNOUT

LIFE CHANGES   UNHAPPINESS WITH JOB

These Stressors will affect your body, mind, emotions and behavior. Check off what you are currently experiencing:

AFFECTS OF STRESS

BODY	MIND
☐ Headaches	☐ Worrying
☐ Frequent infections	☐ Muddled thinking
☐ Taut muscles	☐ Impaired judgment
☐ Muscular twitches	☐ Nightmares
☐ Fatigue	☐ Indecisions
☐ Skin irritations	☐ Negativity
☐ Breathlessness	☐ Hasty decisions

EMOTIONS	BEHAVIOR
☐ Loss of confidence	☐ Accident prone
☐ More fussy	☐ Loss of appetite
☐ Irritability	☐ Loss of sex drive
☐ Depression	☐ Drinking more
☐ Apathy	☐ Insomnia
☐ Alienation	☐ Restlessness
☐ Apprehension	☐ Smoking more

When you are under stress due to life changes or loss, people often will tell you that it just takes time to heal or it is a process. But you may wonder, "What is the process?" In this book, I will attempt to define mine.

The information in this book explains how this simple tool can help you gain stability in your life now, build a firm foundation for the future, and be able to make wise decisions in the moment when you are facing a crisis or making difficult choices.

You will learn clear action steps that reveal your core beliefs, allowing you to build a solid foundation and determine who you are, who you want to become, and what you desire moving forward. It is my wish that you will be helped by using your left hand as a memory tool to move from confusion to clarity. The 5C's work both in highly emotional times and in everyday life.

In the next chapter, I'd like to share how The 5C's came to be by briefly sharing my story. I am eternally grateful that God answered my prayers by giving this tool to me many years ago, as I stood in the hospital after my second suicide attempt. I didn't know that what I discovered that day would evolve into The 5C Solution or that it would help so many others. I couldn't see that far into the future. But now looking back, I can see how clearly these five simple steps have been a Personal Guidance System (PGS) to me and those who have learned it. Now it is my mission to make this method available to the masses so no one will ever feel as alone in their time of need, as I did years ago.

Please connect with me on Facebook and let me know how the 5C Solution makes your path clear! Please see Resources page 167 for a link to my profile.

My Story:
From Chaos to Clarity

"Apparently, something so painful has happened to you that you have buried it deep inside," the doctor said. "It is too painful to recall, so your memory has suppressed it." He was a thin man with a small head and glasses that were too large for his face. The lenses magnified his squinting eyes, making him look like a large bug.

Our two chairs were practically touching in his tiny office. My spine was pressed against the back of the chair as I tried to get as far away from his breath as I could. It stunk like rotting teeth and strong coffee. In the long silence that followed his comment, I realized that I didn't remember how I got into this chair. Bits and pieces of memories were flashing through my brain like an unedited film, but nothing made sense. All I knew was that I felt flatlined, and I just wanted to die. I wanted to go to sleep and never wake up. I wanted the burning in my stomach and the pain in my chest to stop. I wanted to get out of this room and be alone.

"Do you understand where you are?" he asked. I looked away from his stare and glanced down at the shiny brown shoe that was hanging perfectly still at the end of his tightly crossed leg.

I answered in my mind, *Do you understand that I don't want to talk to you?*

After another long silence he said, "We will continue this tomorrow. Try to get some rest. I am here to help you." He continued talking, but I could not stop focusing on his foot and how motionless it hung in space.

When I cross my legs, my foot immediately starts to bounce up and down. My mother used to put her hand on my knee when I was sitting next to her during a meeting at church and say, "Stop making milkshakes." I started to smile at the thought but was quickly brought back to reality when the doctor's sickening breath made my stomach turn. I looked up, and his face was inches from mine, as if he were trying to get into wherever I had been in my thoughts. At this distance, his eyes were huge through his thick glasses. They looked almost comical, but I was in no mood to laugh.

"Where were you just now?" he probed. "Nowhere. Can I go now?" I responded in a whisper. My body felt like a corked bottle. If I talked out loud, the pressure from inside could cause the cork to fly out, and I would explode all over the office.

Finally, the doctor stood, opened the door, and gestured for me to leave. I hadn't remembered coming here or walking into his office. I stood in the doorway and looked around at the large room beyond the office door. Some women were sitting in big, comfortable chairs that formed a half circle facing away from where I stood. A whiteboard was perched on an easel in front of them. A few other women wearing blue hospital gowns were milling around. One was biting her nails as she slowly walked by the chairs; another was sitting and staring into space. The light gray walls seemed to slowly move in and out.

A hand took my elbow and guided me through the room and down a long hallway. A nurse was speaking to me, but I couldn't hear the words, just the sound of someone talking. She opened a door and motioned to a small bed that looked like it belonged in a prison cell. There was a navy blanket and pillow and a folded blue hospital gown placed neatly atop the bed. An identical bed was pushed against the opposite wall and had apparently been slept in because the blanket was in a heap at the foot of the bed and the pillow was lying sideways in the middle. The window at the end of the room was frosted and I could see bars through it on the outside.

Without a moment's hesitation, I pulled down the blanket and crisp white sheet and slid underneath. My knees came to my chest, and I hugged them as I closed my eyes. My body shook from exhaustion, and as I fell asleep, I prayed that I would never wake up.

Except for a small beam of light that shone over my right shoulder, the room was black. I could hear someone walking toward me. A man's shoes appeared in the light beam. I looked up and saw that he was wearing tan shorts and a gray T-shirt. Something in his hand reflected the light and blinded my vision. As the man reached out, I saw that he held a straight razor. My eyes followed it as it came closer and stopped at the top of my bicep.

Suddenly, the blade pierced my skin. I watched as it made a deep cut down the side of my arm. I felt the pain but was unable to move. I screamed inside my mind, but I couldn't open my mouth. Over and over, the blade cut into my naked body. The blood dripped onto the floor, forming a puddle around my feet. He cut into me slowly, silently, and deliberately as I watched.

Who was this man? I needed to know, but when I looked up, his face was missing. There was just a blur of white where his face should be. At that, I unlocked my jaw and started to scream . . .

My eyes flashed open. Someone was shaking me. It took a few seconds to realize that I had just had the nightmare again. I was covered with sweat and had no idea where I was. All I could see was a gray wall staring back at me. Then I heard a girl behind me say, "Wake up. You were dreaming. You started to cry out. Are you okay?" As I rolled over, I realized that I was in the hospital room. Sunlight was shining through the frosted window. I was immediately sad that I hadn't died in my sleep.

This same dream had been happening for months. I think the faceless man represented my ex-husband, and the cutting was how I felt after all the physical, emotional, and spiritual pain that I had endured during the last ten years of our marriage. To the outside world, we had everything. We lived in a beautiful suburb in a new home with a pool, traveled with our two sons, and had parties with our family and friends. No one knew what went on behind closed doors, and I wanted it that way. But the years of pretending that nothing was wrong emotionally devastated me, making life a nightmare. Even though I had figured out the meaning of the dream, it wouldn't go away.

Great, another day to exist, I thought. I rolled over to see a thin girl staring at me, clearly concerned. She wore a bathrobe over a blue hospital gown, and her blonde hair with black roots was swept up into a loose ponytail. She put out her hand and said, "Hi. I'm Kathy. I'm your roomy. You were asleep last night when I came in after dinner, and it's almost noon now. I can't believe they let you sleep in past breakfast and our morning session, but I guess it's because you're new. Man, you must have been exhausted!"

Double great, I thought. *Is she ever going to stop talking?* I sat up and rubbed my eyes. "Listen, you'll be okay," she said. "You're lucky that you have me as a roomy. I've been in and out of these places a dozen times. I'll show you the ropes." *Does she think this is Club Med or something?*

"Where is the bathroom?" I said, interrupting her. "Oh, I'll show you," she said as she swung open the door. She took my arm, escorted me down the hallway and pointed to the restroom door. For a moment I thought she was going to follow me in, so I was relieved when she remained in the hallway. As I stood at the sink to wash my hands, I saw that there weren't any mirrors. Good. I must look like hell. I grasped the sides of the sink and stared into the white bowl. Suddenly I remembered sitting across from my psychiatrist the morning before.

Camden, New Jersey has one of the highest murder and crime rates in the United States, and I live about twenty minutes away in a beautiful suburb. The day before, my psychiatrist had asked me what was wrong, and I had said, "I can't take the pain inside anymore. I'm black and blue on the inside, and no one can see it. Everyone just walks past me like nothing is wrong. Tonight I'm going to drive into Camden at two o'clock in the morning and walk up and down the streets until someone comes along and beats me to a pulp. At least then I'll look on the outside like I feel on the inside."

Oh, so that's how I got here, I thought. Since I had already attempted suicide twice, the doctor had called the ambulance that had brought me here. The long series of traumas that I had experienced over the past decade made me feel like trash, a worthless heap of a woman who had let down everyone I knew and loved, even God. There is no hope after that, and there is nothing anyone could say to me that will convince me otherwise. I was wishing I could wash myself down the drain when I heard the door open and saw a nurse walk in. She put her arm around my waist and guided me back down the hall. I could see the tears dripping from my eyes, but I felt nothing. I was already dead inside.

The nurse took me back to the main room I had seen the night before. I felt nine pairs of eyes watching me as I sat down in one of the soft chairs. The nurse said, "This is Cindy. She arrived last night and will be joining our session." I sat and looked at my hands folded in my lap, avoiding eye contact with anyone. Kathy was sitting next to me and excitedly told everyone that I was her roommate. The doctor sitting by the whiteboard reminded her that she was to focus on her own recovery and then began asking each woman the same questions: How are you feeling today? How are your meds working? What is your assignment for the day? What is your goal?

All the women sounded pathetic, but I couldn't imagine that any of them could possibly feel the way I did. As the session wrapped up, the nurse passed out papers, and gave us an assignment to fill them out before the evening group meeting.

I was hungry, so Kathy showed me to the lunchroom, which looked exactly like an elementary school cafeteria. Long tables with benches attached spanned the room. Snacks, fruits, and drinks were sitting on a countertop at the far end of the room. "You missed breakfast," Kathy said. "The food here is pretty good, although I have to watch everything I eat."

I took a pack of cookies, a banana, and a soda and sat down at one of the tables. Kathy sat across from me. "So, what's your story?" she asked. I looked at her face for the first time. She had huge blue eyes, pale skin, and some acne scars. She could be pretty if she dyed her hair and put on a little makeup. Her cheeks were slightly sunken, and I noticed how thin she was. She looked my age, although I thought I looked younger than my thirty-eight years. I could see that she wasn't going anywhere until I told her something about myself, so I finished the banana and decided to talk.

"I don't even know how to start telling you my story. I feel like I'm living a nightmare that just keeps getting worse. I'm exhausted. It hurts to breathe." Kathy's silence surprised me. Her blue eyes were sucking me in. I needed to talk to someone, and I was tired of doctors. All they ever did was just hand me more prescriptions. Maybe I could trust this stranger with my story and at least get it off my chest.

"I'm going through a divorce," I said. "I've been married since I was eighteen. I never in my wildest imagination thought everything that has happened would be how my life turned out." I could tell by her eyes that she wanted to hear more. "He became an alcoholic. I put up with abuse for years and didn't tell anyone. Then I found out he was cheating on me even though he was an elder in our church. I lost my mind. I had a nervous breakdown. The elders of my church kicked both of us out. They said I wasn't relying on God to help me be strong. My trying to take my life was bringing shame to the religion. Since all my family and friends are in the church, they are all required to shun me until I can prove myself worthy to come back." My eyes never left hers.

"I followed their rules and went to every service, three times a week, with everyone shunning me for almost a year. It was so humiliating. I would just sit and cry at every service. The elders told me I was a distraction so I had to sit in the library by myself.

On the way home I would have to pull over because I was so ashamed of the way people in the church ignored me that I would get sick by the side of the road. At the lowest point of my life, I had no one. Everything I thought was right seems wrong, and everything I thought was wrong can't be right. I don't even know how to live at this point."

That was the most I had said out loud in two days. I felt like my heart had just fallen out of my chest onto the table, exposed and vulnerable. Kathy's expression never changed as she reached across the table and silently hugged me. She sat back onto the bench. I knew she couldn't help me—no one could.

I had never imagined that my life would be such a mess, that I would be on the outside of my religion and rejected by my family and friends. My faith in everything and everyone was ruined. My faith in myself was ruined. Kathy just stared at me blankly. I didn't think she could possibly understand how I was feeling, but it helped to blurt it all out. As I got up and walked away, she sat staring at the place where I had been sitting. I wondered if she even remembered what I had said.

That night at dinner as I stirred my mashed potatoes and black gravy with my fork, I thought about how my world had always been black and white. There was right and wrong—no in-between. If you followed the rules, you were protected from all the evil in the world. God would bless you and guide you. If you broke the rules, all kinds of heartache would result. God would turn His back on you, and you would be alone. How many times had I spoken that simple concept to my husband and kids? You are either on one side of the fence or the other; there was no middle ground. It had to be true. After all, how many times had I seen someone break the rules and then watched as they fell into despair? How could I be on the outside of my religion? My black-and-white world was now swirls of gray. My entire life I believed that being outside my religion was a foreign and scary world, and I had no idea how to exist in it any longer.

I took a bite of the mashed potatoes and gravy. The food was good, but every bite was hard to swallow. My chest felt like a steel drum, and I realized that I was holding my breath for long periods of time. In my peripheral vision I saw that there was activity around me. Some people were talking. Others were getting up and down from the table. Utensils were noisily hitting metal dinner trays. My body seemed like a heavy stone monument of shame as the rest of the world revolved carelessly around me. Surely these "worldly" people couldn't understand.

Kathy came over and asked if I was finished with my tray. As I looked up at her, the tears that had filled my eyes overflowed and ran down my cheeks. "Hey," she said, "you'll be okay. Really." *Will I?* I thought. *No, she has no idea. Nothing will ever be okay again.*

She took my arm and pulled me up. As we walked into the common room, I started to sob uncontrollably. A nurse rushed over and guided me back to my room, where I slumped down onto the bed and covered my head with my arms. How many tears can one person cry? I thought I would have used them all by now, but a new supply kept pouring out.

The nurse came over to me and stroked my back. Quietly, she said, "I think I understand. I saw on your chart that you are a Jehovah's Witness. I have a cousin who was a Witness. Were you disfellowshipped? Is that why you're so devastated?"

Shocked that someone could possibly understand, I looked up and nodded my head. "What am I going to do?" I shouted. The loudness of my voice startled me. I had not meant to say it that intensely.

"You're going to figure out what to do," she said. "That's why you're here."

"But they won't let me back in, and I've let Jehovah God down. I've let my kids down."

"Look," she continued, "I don't know everything about your religion, but I do know that God forgives us when we are sorry for the mistakes we have made. And you certainly look sorry for whatever has happened. He has already forgiven you. Talk to the doctor so that you can forgive yourself."

After she left, I thought about that. Forgive myself. It was a concept that I had not been taught. She was right. I did believe that God forgives us. It was the church elders who had been telling me for the past year that I was not sorry enough or good enough. I started to realize that everything that had happened was not my fault. My self-esteem had been eroded slowly over the years of verbal abuse to the point where I blamed myself for not being able to fix my marriage. The abuse escalated into physical abuse. That wasn't my fault either. I knew I wasn't perfect. I had made a lot of mistakes, but I didn't deserve what had happened to me and I hadn't done anything that was unforgivable. It was men judging me, not God. The cloud of despair started to lift.

The next day was a repeat of the day before. Eat, stand in line for meds, go to the group meeting, and be on time for a private meeting in that tiny office with the psychiatrist with the magnifying glasses on his face. This time the office felt even smaller, and the smell was so wretched that I thought I would be sick. I thought, *Maybe if I just answer his questions really quickly, I can go back to my room.* Unfortunately, there was no quick way of answering questions about what had happened to me.

How could I sum up years of emotional, mental, and physical

abuse? How could I explain that I had hidden it for years so that no one would know that our "perfect" family was really a chaotic mess? How would a person outside my religion ever understand why I was so devastated about being made to leave? People think of Jehovah's Witnesses as a cult. They don't understand why we annoy them by knocking on their doors early in the morning on weekends. Why would my psychiatrist understand that I loved my faith? Instead, I told the doctor that I was feeling much better. I told him that my meds were messed up and made me say crazy things that I did not mean. I forced a smile and asked when I could go home.

"We called your mother," he said.

My eyes grew wide with disbelief. I had forgotten that she was my emergency contact on the medical card in my wallet. A ray of hope filled my heart as I thought that maybe she would now understand how devastated I was, and how sorry. After a long pause, he said flatly, "She refused to come."

As quickly as I had been filled with hope, it was just as quickly dashed. That reality struck so hard that I threw my face into my hands and started to sob again. The doctor said he would order something to calm me down. Did he have to tell me this horrible news? Could he not have just kept it to himself? After all, I was here because I was hurt and humiliated. Were they trying to crush me even further? A nurse came in, led me to the small meds window, and handed me another pill. This time I swallowed it without water. It was getting easier to be numb.

A few minutes later, I found myself sitting in the group session. Suddenly the room started to spin. My heart felt like it was going to jump out of my chest, and I was nauseated. I told Kathy that I had to go lie down and asked her to please check on me in a while because the pill was making me feel weird. It was a good thing I did, because the next thing I knew, I was being rushed to the emergency center. My heart rate had gotten dangerously low.

Kathy later told me that she heard one of the nurses say that I could have died. Hearing that news, I should have been disappointed that I hadn't. After all, I had come in here saying that I wanted the pain to stop; I wanted to fall asleep and never wake up. Instead, I got really mad. I had tried to take my life twice before. Both times I had had my stomach pumped and survived. Now this medication had almost killed me, and here I was again, still alive. I was not mad that it had failed; I was mad that my life was this pathetic. I was angry that this was not the way things were supposed to happen. My ex had taken so many years of my life, and now this craziness was taking time away.

I had a sudden moment of *clarity*. "Okay, God," I said aloud, "I don't know why you don't want me to die, but I'm going to *commit* to figuring it out! If you will help me through the *challenges*, I'm going to *create* a new life, no matter what it takes, and when I'm back on my feet, I will help others do the same, because no one should waste their lives in this much pain and heartache. I want to *celebrate* life again."

The next day was Thanksgiving. A girlfriend whom I had known since I was a teenager ignored our religion's rules and brought my two boys to see me. They arrived with a huge teddy bear and flowers. The group hug from the three of them was the best medicine I could have ever received. My despair had been so profound that I had honestly thought my kids would be better off without me. I figured that if I wasn't here, my mother or sisters would take care of them so that they wouldn't have to suffer from the shunning—but that is not what happened. Instead, my friend somehow found out that I was in the hospital, drove from out of state to be with my kids, and provided them with the care they needed.

As we stood in line in the cafeteria, holding our silver metal trays and waiting for the turkey dinner to be served, I finally felt like I had a reason to be hopeful. I was alive. I had my boys and at least one true friend. I had no idea what was coming next, but I knew I was going to go home and start over. There was nowhere to go but forward.

I didn't know it then, but I had found the formula for The 5C Solution that would help me recover and guide me to rediscover who I was, who I wanted to be, what I wanted, and how to help others do the same. I'm excited to share it with you.

If you are feeling heartbroken, lost, and confused, please know that you are not alone. In fact, this time of your life may be a blessing in disguise. Your circumstances are giving you a reason to pause and find direction. In the next several chapters, I will share with you this amazing tool that you can use as a compass to get clarity. The 5C Solution will create a solid foundation of self-identity and purpose which will give you confidence as you make decisions now and in your future.

Quick Start:
Gaining Control Is at Hand

Life is constantly changing. Things happen that you did not expect or prepare for. How many times have you said, "What am I going to do now?" Losing your job, getting an illness, experiencing the death of a loved one, kids growing up and leaving, finding out you are pregnant, getting divorced, failing a test, retiring—these types of situations can happen at any time, and put you in the position of not knowing what to do next.

When I experienced these changes, I wished I had a simple tool that I could use to navigate through the chaos, quickly gain clarity and know what direction to head with confidence, but I couldn't find such a tool. Instead, I went the usual path of talking to psychologists, psychiatrists, my doctor, friends, family and even strangers. What I came away with were opinions, suggestions and no real answers. It was not until I was at my emotional bottom that day in the hospital that I realized I needed to get to know who I really was and what I really believed.

Years later, when others started asking me how I had pieced my life back together, I began telling my story and explaining the steps I used. I noticed that this tool had five steps, and they all started with the letter C. (I don't think it is a coincidence that my name is Cindy Cipriani—two more C's!) It wasn't until a few years later when I was teaching the steps at a homeless shelter, a resident pointed out that when I taught the process, I would use the finger corresponding to the meaning of each step. Thus using my hand became a memory tool which young and old alike could quickly learn and remember. Since most people have their hands with them all the time, this method became a natural way for them to have The 5C Solution available for quick reference. Finally, an easy tool was born to navigate life's changes.

When you first start learning the steps for the 5C's, you might be tempted to go through them quickly. Resist this temptation and take the time to learn them. Think of it like running a race. Your fastest pace is not at the starting line but occurs after you obtain your stride. The essential part is all the preparation you do before the race to build up to that pace. So, start at the beginning. This system works quickly, but you must be patient. The answers are closer than you think.

We have all heard the expression, "I gotta hand it to you—you did it! High five!" Let's turn that expression into a literal tool to make clear, concise decisions quickly and easily. Using your hand to remember The 5C Solution, you are equipped with a tool to walk through any perplexing problem in your life, relationships or business.

A Brief Description of The 5Cs

The following is a short description of the 5C steps and how to remember them on your left hand.

Step 1: Clarity. This step is represented by the pinky. Even though it is the smallest finger, it is the most important place to start. Starting without clarity would be like trying to get to a destination with no address to program into your GPS: you wouldn't get anywhere. This step will guide you to figure out who you are, who you want to be, and what you want.

You will learn more about clarity in Chapter 1.

Step 2: Commitment. This step is represented by the ring finger. Once you have clarity, you must commit to making changes.

Do you know why wedding rings are worn on the ring finger of the left hand? The Romans thought we had a vein that went from this finger—which they called the "love" finger—directly to the heart, so it became a custom to wear wedding rings on this finger.

When people get married, they usually have a ceremony during which they declare their commitment to each other before their friends and relatives. In America, we do this for two reasons: one is that couples want to celebrate their love, and another is that they want to make a public commitment and declaration that they are now bonded. This public declaration also holds the couple accountable.

There is a huge difference between saying you want something and being committed to getting it. You could compare it to the difference between a weekend warrior who plays a sport occasionally and tries to be good at it, and an Olympic athlete. Who would you say is more committed? Everything the Olympic athlete does—their daily activities, their diet, how they spend their time and money, how much rest they get—is in alignment with obtaining their goal.

To obtain what you want, you will need to have determination and make consistent choices. Something that will help keep you on course is to make a public declaration of your commitment. It does not have to be in front of a group of people; you can choose one person to be your cheerleader. Select someone who will not only keep you accountable but will encourage you to stay on pace and not give up. (A word of caution: Do not choose a person who will nag, discourage, or voice negative comments to you. Choose wisely by choosing someone whose opinion you respect.)

You can choose different people for different goals, so start thinking about who you will choose when we get to that action step.

There is one commitment you should make right this minute: make a commitment to complete this book. Tell a friend. Invite them to go through this with you.

You will learn more about commitment in Chapter 2.

Step 3: Challenges. This step is represented by the middle finger. Have you ever noticed that as soon as you commit to something, life can throw you the middle finger? That is why this finger represents challenges.

Challenges are both external and internal. The internal challenges are usually the ones that beat us up the most. To prepare, you need to determine what thoughts could keep you from achieving your goals and what to do when you start thinking them. This will enable you to be prepared. Instead of being caught off guard, you will welcome the challenge and be able to smile and say, "I know exactly what to do now. I've already planned for this."

You will learn more about challenges in Chapter 3.

Step 4: Creation of a plan. This step is represented by the pointer finger. This finger faces away from you, thus pointing to the future.

After obtaining clarity and committing to making the changes necessary to overcome your challenges, you may ask yourself, "Now what? How do I get from where I am to where and who I want to be?" Perfect question!

French author and aviator Antoine de Saint-Exupéry is credited with the popular saying, "A goal without a plan is just a wish." In order to move forward, you need to create a plan, and doing so is much easier than you might imagine. Of course, you want to go from right now, in your state of chaos, directly to your goal as soon as possible. However, there are steps in between that are important for you to take.

Having a plan will accomplish two things for you:

1. You will have an actionable series of steps that will be your guide or roadmap.
2. Setting smaller accomplishments and achieving them will give you enthusiasm, confidence, and the power to continue until your final goal is achieved.

You will learn how to create a plan in Chapter 4.

Step 5: Celebrate! This step is represented by the thumbs-up gesture, which stands for congratulations, approval, and your happiness with an outcome. Step 5 is all about celebration.

Most people imagine celebrating after they reach their final goal, but they often forget to acknowledge the steps they took to get there. Goals aren't met in one giant leap. They are accomplished by taking one action or step at a time. However, each step is important because it gets you closer to where you want to be.

Sir Isaac Newton described the importance of movement when he published the first law of motion in 1687 after he discovered that "an object in motion tends to remain in motion." By taking the first step toward your goal, and then the next, and then the next, you will develop a new habit that will keep you moving. But notice that Newton said an object "tends" to stay in motion. That means that even though you get started, there can be a tendency to stop before you get to your goal. This is because we can become inactive if we aren't motivated. Celebrating every step along the way is the secret to *wanting* to keep moving until the new habit is formed and the ultimate goal is achieved. We humans run from pain and toward pleasure, so we can trick our minds to focus on pleasure by rewarding ourselves with fun activities when we accomplish even small strides.

You may not be having much fun in your life at this point, but don't worry; soon you will be celebrating small accomplishments regularly, which will not only propel you forward but will have you jumping out of bed in the morning ready to take on the day so that you can celebrate again.

You will learn more about celebrating in Chapter 5.

Now that you know what each finger represents, let's get started with The 5C Solution to create your clear path.

PART I

The 5C Solution

CHAPTER 1

Clarity

Clarity is essential. Knowing exactly what you want
builds your self-confidence immeasurably.

—BRIAN TRACY

Since you are reading this book, you are probably at a crossroad
in your life. When emotions run high, it's hard to see the choices
you have, let alone the right ones to choose. In order to make
the right decisions, you must gain clarity on your situation, and
in order to gain clarity, you must stop—like this familiar hand
signal instructs.

Yes, just pause. When you are feeling confused or overwhelmed, just hold up your
hand as a reminder to take a moment to step
back from the emotions and breathe deeply.
Have you been holding your breath?

We are emotional beings, and when our emotions run high, we often hold our breath. Taking a few deep breaths will flood your brain with oxygen, which helps you think more clearly and calms down the triggers that can lead to panic or frustration. Take a few seconds to breathe deeply three times. Notice how this calms your emotions and allows your logic to take over. Now you are ready to gain clarity. Remember to stop and breathe anytime you start becoming emotional, unfocused or overwhelmed. Are you ready to dive in?

In this chapter, you will get clear about who you are spiritually, physically, mentally, and emotionally. You will evaluate the relationships, people, places, and possessions in your life right now. Then you will review your attitude on prosperity, your purpose, who you want to be, and what you want.

Expressions such as "I feel like I have no direction" and "I feel lost" may feel like having a GPS without a defined destination. If you don't know where to go, you will feel stuck. When you feel stuck and confused because your life is in chaos, you must pull to the side of life's highway and recalculate the reason.

In order to move out of the chaos, you must have clarity about three things: who you are, who you want to be, and what you want. Before you can begin to move forward in the right direction with your life and take your first step to gaining true clarity, you must find the answers to these questions.

Clarity begins with digging deep; getting to the root of not just the problem you are currently facing but *who you are* as a person. How often do you take time to really explore your core beliefs? Usually this happens when you come to an incredibly difficult and emotional time in your life. To remodel your life after a traumatic event, you will need to take apart your thoughts, analyze why you believe what you do, and formulate a plan, much like having an architect draw the elements of a building. You must start with the foundation, laying the blocks and reinforcing them for the load that will sit on top. Knowing this about yourself is the road map for every decision you will make and action you will take. The reason people get stuck and are unable to figure out how to move forward is because they are on uncharted territory after a crisis.

Doing this clarity work may sound overwhelming. After all, you want a quick solution, not to dig into the portals of your soul, right? Don't worry, you will be okay. Breathe. Using the 5C's will make figuring out your unique and authentic self easier because it will serve as a guide. Instead of a GPS, the 5C's become what I call your PGS (Personal Guidance System)!

I have a professional background in the home renovation industry, and the 5C tool reminds me of when someone has had damage to their house due to an accident, flood or fire. The obvious damage could be repaired. However, if a thorough inspection of the foundation for structural damage has not been done, the repair will only be temporary and superficial. When your life has been torn apart by the end of a relationship, the loss of a loved one, loss of a job, or anything that shakes you to your core, it may feel like your foundation has been damaged. In order to rebuild your life, getting clarity on your core beliefs will help you make solid choices that are in harmony with who you are now. This will enable you to make wise choices as your life expands forward into the future. If you already know your core beliefs and have been building your life on them, when something traumatic happens it will be easier for you to recover. But if you do not know why you believe something or even what to believe, then a traumatic event can be like a tidal wave hitting a shore house. If your house is reinforced with steel pier footings that are bored down to bedrock, it will withstand the force; but if it is built on the sand, it will wash away. Even Jesus gave the example of building on rock instead of sand.

Subconsciously everything you decide is based on your belief system, which is based on your individual view of the world. Your experiences have taught you lessons that have become the basis for what you believe to be fact. When you are faced with any decision, your brain goes deep into your emotional experience vault and pulls out the lessons you have learned from your past. What you decide today is affected by things that have happened to you since your birth. Most researchers agree that a child's belief system is fairly well established by the age of six. By the age of fifteen, due to their life experiences, most teens have definite values, beliefs, and judgments subconsciously programmed into their minds.

This explains so much about people. Children interpret the world by observation before they can even talk. They watch and soak up every movement, comment, and action the adults around them make. They register this as the way things should be because they adore and trust the adults in their lives. The adult behavior they see becomes their "normal," and thus they mimic their parents' behavior. This explains why so many people repeat the mistakes of their parents.

My mother used to say, "The world doesn't revolve around you!" She was wrong. My world does revolve around me. I am the only one looking at the world through my eyes. You are the only one who looks at the world through your eyes. No one else will ever have your exact experiences, emotions or interpretations of them. They have formed who you are, how you react and why you think the way you do.

If you were raised in a household full of anger, fighting, name calling, and abuse, you will likely choose a mate who mimics that behavior even if you made a conscious effort not to repeat this negative behavior. Being in that type of relationship and holding on to it can feel familiar and normal, even though you know it is not right. This is because your belief system was formed when you were young and impressionable. Amazing, isn't it?

The brain is a complex computer. Whatever information goes in is processed, attached to an emotion and filed away. Your internal program is as unique as you are. The only way to achieve real clarity on the path you wish to take is to stop and analyze each facet of your being. Remember, powerful life lessons were learned when you were a small child. Patterns of communication and behavior are stored that influence your reactions when you are an adult.

Have you ever had someone say something that reminded you of something that happened when you were young, and suddenly you felt as though you were back in that moment? In a split second your brain retrieved that memory and presented it to you, even when you hadn't thought about it for decades.

I was the middle child in our family. My older sister was labeled "the smart one." My younger sister was "the cute one." I felt invisible most of the time. I did not feel like I fit in anywhere. One day, as I looked at the three baby photographs of us hanging on the stair wall of the house I grew up in, I asked my mother why my sisters were in frilly dresses and I was dressed in a boy's shorts and top. She said, "Oh, you were supposed to be a boy." It suddenly hit me why I became a tomboy. I had been labeled as such from before I could even remember.

While my sisters were dainty and feminine, my dad took me under his wing teaching me to fix cars, mow the lawn, garden and do home repairs. I dressed for hard work and didn't wear jewelry or makeup because I was used to getting greasy and dirty working around the house. My tomboy label was how I proved myself worthy of my parents' love. My older sister rebelled as a teenager, so I tried to be the "good" daughter. I tried to be the perfect Christian. It just seemed like nothing I did was noticeable. Feeling invisible became part of my belief system, so decisions I made as an adult were tainted by my feelings of invisibility and inadequacy. To this day, whenever I feel left out or hurt, the little voice in my head whispers, "You don't matter. No one cares how you feel. You probably did something to cause this." In that moment I become the little girl jumping up and down, trying to be noticed, loved and accepted.

I now realize that this was my "story," and like a fairytale, it was not true. It was my interpretation of the labels that were given to me as a child. I was in control to change those labels any time I wished, but for many years I based my choices on feeling not as intelligent or attractive as my siblings. I also put up with abuse because I blamed myself. Because I was in a religion where I was taught to not question authority, to be submissive to men and to hide misconduct in fear of being judged or shunned, I did not know who I really was. I didn't formulate my own opinions. I just believed and followed the rules.

You may be at a point in your life where you don't know who you truly are. Perhaps you are or have been in a relationship where the other person's wants, needs or behaviors molded you into someone you hardly recognize. You may be just going through the motions, doing things you hate but going along with them anyway. You may be experiencing physical manifestations of not being true to who you really are, such as having headaches, stomachaches, depression, anxiety or lacking zest for life.

If any of this sounds familiar, know that there is a way out of the darkness, and The 5C Solution is the tool you need. It wasn't until I did this clarity work that I discovered that I liked being feminine, wearing makeup and jewelry. I also discovered that not only was I strong physically but mentally. I could form my own opinions and I liked finding out who I truly am.

Let's start right now by finding out who you truly are. And in case you don't know yet, you are a magnificent, unique, fabulous person!

You will find worksheets throughout the book to help you process the steps. You may be thinking, "I don't like writing things down and doing exercises. I just want answers." These types of thoughts will block your progress. Just do your best to ignore them and use the worksheets to write down your responses. Remind yourself that you are longing to relieve your pain and stress to get answers. Writing down your thoughts and goals will bring clarity and the success you are seeking. It is amazing how written goals have a way of coming true. That is why successful businesses write business plans.

Spoken words disappear. Written words remain, can be referenced, and are a foundation to action. When you put your desires to paper, you show the universe that you mean what you say, that you have thought through what you want. Your brain is then programmed to search out what it needs to fulfill your desires. You may not know how it will happen yet, but that will come later.

Get a pen, and let's get started.

To achieve true clarity, take some time to reflect on the following three questions.

- ☞ Who are you right now?
- ☞ Who do you want to be?
- ☞ What do you really want?

Now let's take a deep dive into who you are.

Who You Are

Few of us stop to examine who we really are until something drastic happens in our life. Until then, we just go through our days providing for ourselves and our families. We have things to do, people to see, bills to pay. We may feel that we are just fine. But we change over time, and what we believed years ago may have changed because of new information, circumstances, or influences.

Just yesterday Rose, a woman in her eighties who recently lost her husband of fifty-two years, came to see me. Tears filled her eyes as she said, "I don't know who I am now." Rose had defined herself as part of a couple for so long that she was unsure of who she was as an individual. Is that how you feel?

The following section provides a vital exercise to help you gain your own individual and unique clarity. It may seem overwhelming or too much work at first, but you will be able to do it without much thought or time. Don't make it complicated. There is no need to put pressure on yourself to come up with answers. Just answer honestly about what comes to mind when you think of each area.

To begin, let's break your life into five areas: spiritual, physical, mental, emotional, and relationships. After you read about each of the areas, ask yourself the following questions.

- ☞ What do I believe?
- ☞ Who taught this to me? When?
- ☞ Where was I when I started believing this?
- ☞ Why did I believe it?
- ☞ How do I feel about it now as it meshes with my current life knowledge and experience?
- ☞ Do I still believe this to be true?

Let's look at each of the five areas and see what they mean.

SPIRITUAL

In this section, your spirit is comprised of your belief system, core values, energy, and how you contribute to the world. It comes first because these are your foundation.

People often equate spirituality with religion. That was my perspective years ago, too. However, my definition changed as I saw some deeply religious people act in selfish and hypocritical ways, while others who had no religious affiliation gave of themselves and their resources in remarkable ways. That is now my personal clarity on the definition of "spiritual." You are entitled to yours and this is the time to formulate your definition of spirituality.

We do, however, need to bring up the subject of religion because many of us are deeply affected by the teachings of the religions in which we were raised. All religions have fundamental beliefs that, if followed, are a guide to the believer's behavior.

Learning rules from the Bible such as you should not steal, you should treat others the way you want to be treated, and do not judge your brother are obviously good basic actions for society. There are thousands of religions that base their beliefs on other sacred books and teachings. If you examine specific teachings and controversial doctrines, you will see that individuals believe many variations of doctrine even within the same religion or congregation. So spirituality as referred to here goes beyond religion.

I believe you owe it to yourself to take time to examine exactly what *you* believe, not just what you have been *told* to believe. This is because you are probably subconsciously following your inherited belief system. Guilt often manifests when we do something contrary to what we were taught. We do something because we want to do it, and we obviously believe that it is okay to do in the moment—until our conscience starts pricking us with thoughts from teachings we have learned.

If you are behaving in a way that is opposite from a foundational belief, you will feel it in your body. You tense up. Your stomach may hurt, or you will start getting physically ill. When this happens, you have two options: 1) change your behavior to match your belief, or 2) change your belief.

It takes effort to change a belief. You must dig deep and ask yourself these questions:

- ☛ What have I been taught is right in this situation?
- ☛ Do I believe that?
- ☛ If I am behaving differently from that belief, why?
- ☛ Am I covering up emotions that I don't know how to deal with?
- ☛ Have my beliefs changed?

One of my clients, Denise, was brought up by strict Catholic parents. Denise was sent to Catholic school. She grew up being told, and therefore believes, that sex before marriage is wrong. However, she has been having sex with various boyfriends for several years. When she engages in this activity, she hears a little voice in the back of her mind saying, *You shouldn't be doing this.* Her need for closeness and the physical enjoyment outweigh the voice in the moment.

Denise is not consciously thinking this now, but she has begun to have stomach pain and headaches on a regular basis. She has been to a doctor, and he cannot find anything physically wrong. He tells her to stop eating acidic foods, reduce stress, and take headache medication. The symptoms subside for a few days or weeks, and she goes back to her normal routine. However, she still feels like something is wrong. She lacks energy and enjoyment in life.

While doing clarity work with me, Denise discovered that these symptoms are part of a pattern that occurs only after she has sex. Does she still believe that having sex before marriage is wrong?

There are three options:

Option 1. After thinking about it, she decides that she does believe sex before marriage is wrong. She has been acting against a fundamental belief, and the guilt is manifesting itself physically. She wants to be in alignment spiritually, so she asks her current boyfriend if he is interested in marriage. He says he is, and they begin planning to be married soon. She tells him that she wants to stop having sex until they are married. The headaches and stomach problems disappear. She is happy and aligned with her core beliefs.

Option 2. After thinking about it, she decides that she does believe sex before marriage is wrong. She has been acting against a fundamental belief, and the guilt is manifesting itself physically. She decides that she wants to be in alignment spiritually, so she asks her current boyfriend if he is interested in marriage. He says no. Although disappointed, she realizes his values are not the same as hers, and she breaks off the relationship to find someone who will respect her beliefs.

Option 3. After examining her belief system, she realizes that she does not believe having sex before marriage is wrong; she understands that she does not agree with this religious rule. She sees that she can overrule the previous teaching in order to spiritually align with her personal beliefs. To do this, she openly acknowledges her new belief, that it is okay to have sex prior to marriage. Denise reprograms her belief system accordingly, thus alleviating any guilt associated with the behavior.

Can you see how our beliefs can affect our decisions and even our health?

You may ask how you determine what your fundamental beliefs are, and I have an answer: you create a book of your beliefs.

My Book of Cindy

When I was removed from my religion, the foundation of my spiritual life was rocked to the core. I had totally believed that I was in the one and only true religion, and there was a certain peace of mind that came with that thinking. Being convinced that my beliefs were correct grounded me, and there was no need to question them. When others found themselves in trouble,

I would simply look at their problems and think, *Well, if they followed the rules, they wouldn't be in that situation.*

To me, everything was black and white with no gray middle ground. I became highly judgmental and did not allow for human imperfection or diversity of thought. As a result, when I found myself thrown off the righteous highway of my religion and into a ditch, I had to examine not only what had happened to me and why I made the mistakes I made, but also every core belief I had. In order to do that, I started what I called *My Book of Cindy.* Many of the books in the Bible are named after a person, so I thought I would write my own translation of my core beliefs as I now understood them.

For the next several months, I wrote down fundamental thoughts after the words "I believe . . ." Doing this was like painting a picture of my soul. For the first time in my life, I dared to question. I pushed myself beyond the confines of what I was taught and into a realm of curiosity. I became fascinated with other people's beliefs as we discussed them—how they came to their conclusions and how they now act in accordance to them. The walls of judgment started to melt as I realized that each of us can form our own opinions. What makes us different is that we all act the way we decide to act, and our actions may or may not be in accordance with a belief standard that we were taught. In 1856, Abraham Lincoln said, "Actions speak louder than words." I find this to be true, as actions do reveal a person's true beliefs.

If you say you believe one action to be true but are doing the opposite, you do not really believe in the truth of the first action. You say you believe it simply because somewhere in your history you were taught what is "right and wrong," and that belief fell into the "right" category.

Truly knowing *what you believe* and *who you are* will bring you into alignment with your own spirit. Your spirit changes, as do your values, based on experiences and knowledge. Being up to date with your current beliefs is essential in order to be grounded in your decisions and the direction you go in life.

EXERCISE

Get a fresh tablet or notebook. Write My Book of (your name) on the cover.

At the top of each page, write "I believe," and begin recording your fundamental beliefs—the things you know for sure are true.

Don't get distracted with trying to think of every single belief. This is just a tool that you work with gradually as you gain more clarity. For example, after you hear about a controversial topic, take a few moments to consider what you believe about it and why, and then write it down in your book.

After you have done the exercise and have several entries on what you believe, you can watch the picture unfold of who you really are right now. As new realizations arise, continue to write down what you believe.

I continue to write in *My Book of Cindy* whenever a thought truly resonates with me. The book has become an essential tool I use to revisit my core beliefs. Whenever a subject comes up that I am not sure about, I research, ponder, and explore. When I reach a conclusion that resonates with my soul, I write another page in *My Book of Cindy*. There are times when I am introduced to new information that changes what I believed before. When that happens, I smile and write down why my opinion has changed.

The information in this book is solely for your benefit. You can share it with others if you wish, but there is no need to defend your beliefs or try to push them on others. There is an expression, "If you stand for nothing, you can fall for anything." If you do not know what you believe and why, the strong beliefs and opinions of others can influence you to do things about which you feel uncomfortable. The goal is to come to a place of nonjudgment; a place of understanding, peace, and contentment within yourself that will give you a solid foundation as a basis for your decisions and actions.

We are like trees. As we grow our root systems, we need to dig deeper into the soil for stability and nourishment. If we remain shallow, we can be uprooted when storms blow through. When unexpected turmoil arises in life, we often feel devastated because, even though we are adults, we have not taken the time to establish a strong foundation. Our self-worth is based on other people's opinions or someone else's preference. Writing your book of core values and beliefs will give you deep roots to withstand life's storms and become a shelter to those around you.

Any time you are asked your opinion and you respond, "I don't know," your soul is telling you that it needs more information to form an opinion. This is part of the work of gaining clarity. Your core values are part of the spirit that feeds your soul and guides your direction in life. It is essential that you know who you are, what enriches your spirit, and what areas you should focus on to improve and give back. We will explore this in greater detail later.

PHYSICAL

Stand in front of a full-length mirror, and take a close look at your physical body. What condition are you currently in? Are you healthy? Are you hydrated? Do you exercise and strengthen your muscles? We all know we are our own worst critic, and there are things about ourselves we wish were different. However, right now we are gaining clarity on reality. Who are you physically right now? To achieve clarity, be factual, not judgmental, about your current state.

Record your physical data in Worksheet 1. Once you have filled in the data, you will have a physical assessment of the mechanics of the container that is carrying you every day. Your body is unique. Think about that. No one will ever be you. So you don't need to compare yourself to anyone else.

Much of your health is based on your choices and decisions regarding your food and exercise. Every time you put something into your mouth, you are making a choice. Are you fueling the amazing mechanical system that is your human body, or are you giving it something that will eventually hurt it in some way?

When I talk with my clients about their physical body, one of the complaints I hear most often is that most of them "want" to lose weight but can't seem to do so. We all know there is only one way to do that: food choices and exercise. The health and diet industries are multimillion-dollar businesses that offer many ways to go about eating fewer calories and burning stored fat.

If you have become clear about wanting to change your body in any way, Chapter 6 will help you. For now, if you didn't do it earlier, go back and write down the facts about your body as they are presently, with no judgment, in Worksheet 1.

Worksheet 1. Physical Data

MY PHYSICAL DESCRIPTION		
Height		
Weight		
Waist Measurement		
Blood Pressure		
Cholesterol (LDL/HDL)		
Check one:	HEALTHY	NEEDS IMPROVEMENT
Hair		
Skin		
Teeth		
Eyesight		
Hearing		
Body Fat		
Pain Level		
Muscle Tone		
Sleep		
Digestion		
Joints		
Energy Level		
Overall Health		

MENTAL

The brain is our control center. Getting clear about how and what you think about is essential. It sounds funny to think about what you think about, but we often do not realize how our thoughts take us in a life direction different from what we desire. Knowing what is important to you and why will alleviate stress, help attract like-minded companions and relationships, and even allow you to have more fun in life. It all begins with those thoughts that whirl around in your head.

Your Negative Voice

All of us have voices inside our heads. You have certainly heard of the description of an angel sitting on one shoulder and the devil on the other. The angel whispers positive affirmations in one ear, while the devil shouts negative and demeaning reasons in the other ear *not* to listen to the angel. Doesn't it seem that the negative voice is so much louder? Who knows why we have these two voices, but when you get clear about something you want to achieve, these voices are why making it happen is not a piece of cake. You start out thinking, "Yes. I am going to accomplish this!" but then that negative voice immediately begins droning, "You can't do that! You aren't smart enough, good enough, don't have enough . . ."

I invented a unique way to handle this negative inner voice: I named it. I call my inner negative voice "Mr. Prickly" because it pricks at me. I also wanted to give it a male name because, mentally, it helps me remember that it is a distinctly separate entity from me. The great thing about this separate entity is that I can tell it to shut up! I don't have to feel like I am beating myself down. I can just figuratively walk away.

Do you have that one person in your life who constantly gives you a list of reasons why things won't work? How much time do you spend with them? Hopefully as little as possible. You are with your Mr. Prickly 24/7, but you can take control and shut him down. This is totally possible and even enjoyable when you begin practicing. At first it will feel like you are talking to yourself (which you are), but being aware that you have control of your thoughts is empowering. Every negative statement your Mr. Prickly throws at you is just a challenge for you to answer.

Take a minute now to name your negative inner voice. This one action will change your life!

I have a client who calls her inner voice "Ants" because she feels like her thoughts are crawling everywhere. Another client calls her inner voice "Negative Nancy," and a young man named his "Cersei" after a villain in *Game of Thrones*. Use your imagination to come up with a name that reminds you that you control this negative voice, it does not control *you*.

Education

One more area of mental clarity is your education or learning level. From the time you were born, your mind has been programmed with new information. As a child you learned how to get your basic needs met. You also observed the way the adults in your life handled emotions, loss, and communication. Their actions were what you eventually interpreted as normal.

As you grew and went to school, new skills such as reading, writing, and math became fundamental knowledge. You may have gone on to college and studied a specific area of education. At some point you probably stopped going to school, went to work, and continued to learn on the job. Learning never stops;

it just takes on different forms. Ask yourself if you are satisfied with your current level of education. What mental stimulation is your brain craving?

I have found that intelligent people who are bored often fill their lives with habits that are destructive. These habits, such as gambling, smoking, drinking excessively and so on, fill a need to do something. If you have such habits, you can occupy your time by feeding your mind with new information so you can truly break free. Learning a new language or hobby, for example, is mentally stimulating and makes life more interesting. It works!

EMOTIONAL

How are you feeling? Do you control your emotions or do they control you? Attaining clarity about our emotions unlocks the key to our power.

Consider Mr. Spock from *Star Trek*. He is all logic, no emotions. When there is some kind of crisis on the Starship Enterprise, the humans run around in panic while Mr. Spock calmly stands by, stating the logical answer to their problem. When I first saw this character, I thought how nice it would be to not get caught up in emotions like sadness, fear, and anger. But we also see that because he has no emotions, he doesn't enjoy some of life's most precious gifts, such as rejoicing over accomplishments or falling in love.

We are humans with a vast array of emotions, and they always trump logic. We think with our minds but make decisions based on how our heart feels, because the heart is the seat of emotion. We carry our emotions in our torso. I'm sure you have said things such as, "My stomach is tied in knots," "My heart is breaking," and "I feel like I have an elephant sitting on my chest." We feel physical sensations from the emotional turmoil we experience.

When I ask what my clients want to accomplish in their coaching, the most prevalent response I hear is "balance and peace." When I dig deeper, they tell me their emotions are "all over the place." One of my best friends calls this *spinning*. This is a great word to describe this situation, because when our emotions are all over the place, we spin out of control. Everything becomes a whirlwind of feelings, and we are not grounded, calm, or content.

You can achieve clarity about your emotions by taking note of the way you are feeling right now and figuring out what questions need answers. Some emotions you may feel are anxiety, guilt, heartbreak, anger, and uncertainty. Do any of these feelings sound familiar? If so, are they clouding your judgment? Is it hard to see a way forward beyond these overwhelming emotions?

When you get clear on how overwhelming emotions can override your better nature, you will start to feel them calm down. The more questions you answer, the more balanced, focused, and grounded you will become. Doing this work is essential for not only getting through your current situation, but also for moving forward by laying the groundwork for how you respond to unexpected future events.

RELATIONSHIPS

In order to gain clarity in your life, it is vital that you understand the quality of the various types of relationships you have. In this section, you will explore your relationships with people, places, possessions, prosperity, and purpose.

People

The people in your life directly impact how you deal with crisis or trauma. Let's take a deeper look at your personal relationships.

You may have someone in your life—a parent, sibling, child, or spouse—with whom you wish you were closer or think you should be closer but are not, and the distance may gnaw at you. Even if you think you are fine with the relationship being contentious, you may find yourself looking at similar relationships between other people who are loving and close, and wish you had the same thing.

Right now, make a list of the names of the closest people in your life in Worksheet 2. Beside each name, enter their relationship to you, then enter a number between 0 and 10 that represents the status of your relationship at present, using the scale of 0 = no relationship and 10 = extremely close and loving. Be honest in your evaluations.

For instance, my mother and sisters have not spoken to me in more than twenty years. While I have come to accept that they are doing this because of their religious beliefs and there is nothing I can do to change it, when I see other mothers and daughters shopping together and enjoying each other's company, my heart aches. I wish things were different. My "zero" hurts.

Worksheet 2. People in My Life

NAME	RELATIONSHIP TO ME	RELATIONSHIP STATUS, 0 TO 10

Once you have finished this, write down why you gave each relationship the rating you did, and what you would like the relationship to be. For example, do you have a 3 next to your spouse and wish it were an 8? Why? We will explore how to make these changes happen later. For the time being, simply record your responses.

Places

Are you attached to certain places? It may seem odd to have a relationship with a place, but we often feel "at home" in specific locations. When we move away from our hometown or state, we may experience a grieving period because we have left familiar surroundings. Our daily routines change, and change can be emotionally hard. Even when you had planned on and looked forward to moving, unexpected periods of sadness can creep in. This is normal. Our level of security is built into the familiarity of our surroundings.

Think about how attached you are to your house, town, state, or country. Write down a list of places where you are most comfortable.

_____

_____

_____

_____

_____

_____

_____

Possessions

Have you ever seen a five-year-old carrying their worn and tattered baby blanket? Unless you are the parent trying to break your child of the habit, you probably looked at them and said, "Aw, how cute!"

As adults, we can also become very attached to possessions. Today, young and old alike are glued to their technology. Looking down at smart phones has become the new posture. Families sitting in restaurants and staring at their cell phones with no eye contact or conversation is the new normal.

Analyze how much virtual time you spend with your virtual friends. Are you obsessed? When you made your list of people in your life who are important to you, did you list any virtual friends? Are your real, live, in-person relationships suffering? Do you find yourself less talkative, never using the phone to talk to people, and spending most of the time alone, texting?

Achieving clarity on exactly how much of your day is spent online, and recognizing how hard it would be to reign in your need to post to your social media, can be quite eye-opening. Clarity on this issue can help you find time to do the things you really want to do, such as finding answers to the problems you are facing.

As an exercise, track the next forty-eight hours to see how much time you spend online. This is easy with an app on your phone.

Date:_____ Hours:_____ Minutes:_____

We are attached to other possessions besides our phones and tablets, too. Do you share your possessions easily with others, or do you keep them to yourself? Are there possessions that belong to your parents or family members that you would fight over in the future? If you were to lose your house in a fire, what are the things you would miss the most? Would you have a difficult time adjusting to living somewhere else? Ask yourself why these things mean so much to you.

Another relationship we have is with our habits. If you smoke, drink, gamble, or otherwise engage in addictive habits, how hard would it be to give them up?

Prosperity

This section on clarity would not be complete without mentioning your attitude about prosperity—in other words, money. Everyone has a relationship with money. It is strange that money is such a huge part of our lives but that most people are guarded about discussing their personal finances.

What is your relationship to money? What is your financial background story? The way you grew up may subconsciously steer your decisions and your current financial position.

If you were poor when you were young, do you always feel like you never have enough? Do you want your family to have more than you did when you were growing up? Does this desire drive you to work harder, achieve more, or buy more possessions in the effort to be happy? Many parents say that they want their kids to have all the things they did not have. They want them to have it easier than they did, so they will shower them with gifts, trips, cars, and college educations to the point of racking up debt just so the kids have it good. Are the kids better off?

Blogger Erin Kurt wrote a terrific article about the top ten things that students around the world love most about their mothers. They include giving hugs, spending one-on-one quality time snuggling under a blanket and watching a movie together, eating nutritious food at dinner, and talking about how to have fun on the weekend. I love this list because it shows that what kids value is their relationship with their parents, not the material possessions. (See Lifehack.org, https://www.lifehack. org/articles/featured/the-top-10-things-children-really-want-their-parents-to-do-with-them.html.)

If you were raised without want, how has that affected your relationship to money? Do you feel pressure to do better than your parents, or has it made you feel like there is no way you could be more successful than they are, so why try? Or something in between?

We all need money to buy food, clothing, and shelter. However, the world we live in today has much more to offer than just those essentials. There is a tape running in the back of your mind where your view on finances is stored, and you may not even be aware of it. Gaining clarity on the contents of that tape will help you figure out why you are not content, motivated, able to slow down, or always feel inadequate.

Use Worksheet 3 to calculate your current financial net worth. Be totally honest, and don't judge yourself. Just write the facts. We will refer back to with this information later.

Worksheet 3. Your Financial Net Worth

MONTHLY INCOME AFTER TAXES		
	$	
	$	
	$	
x12 = Total Yearly Income		$
ASSETS:		
Home	$	
Car	$	
Savings	$	
Other	$	
TOTAL ASSETS:		$
TOTAL INCOME & ASSETS:		$
DEBTS:		
Monthly Expenses x 12	$	
Loans	$	
Credit Card Debt	$	
TOTAL DEBT:		$
TOTAL NET WORTH:		$
(Subtract Debt from Total Income & Assets)		

Purpose

You may be emotionally tied to your job, the place you work or the title on your business card. Because we spend so much of our time working, we can become emotionally identified with what we do instead of who we are.

I often see this attachment when someone is facing retirement or has recently retired. Even those who count down the days until they are "free" often feel totally lost without the daily routine once they are retired. I see this especially so in those who retire from management positions; they face not knowing how to go through life without overseeing someone or something. Suddenly having no responsibility or visible accomplishments can be depressing and disconcerting. Many spouses complain that their newly retired spouse is always "bossing them around" or "trying to manage" their lives. Too much togetherness can test any relationship when you are used to being apart most of the day, especially with someone who is struggling to find themselves after retirement.

Stay-at-home moms and dads face a similar dilemma when their children grow up. They struggle with the question, "What do I do now?" Our culture deeply undervalues the job of working at home that some mothers and fathers choose. When the children grow up, the stay-at-home parent is left without a résumé or work history, and they are trapped in the fear of moving forward with a life that is now so different. The idea of lacking a title on a business card can hold them back from moving forward into a new career. Their role has changed from being needed all the time to not being needed on a daily basis. They can be emotionally attached to the relationship they had with their children when the kids were younger because it fulfilled them.

Now they may question their purpose. This dilemma falls under the "Purpose" category because it refers to life roles, but it also falls under the "Relationship" category because our relationships with our grown children are different from when they were little, and that surely takes adjustment.

If you think, "I'm trying to find my purpose and don't know what it is," you are not alone. Almost everyone I have spoken with about this is not really sure what their purpose in life is. Even broaching the subject can bring up strong emotions. Older people can feel like they are running out of time to figure it out. Younger people feel like they need to know *now* so that they don't spend time going in the wrong direction.

Why do we all feel the need for a purpose? Perhaps it is because we are complex and intelligent human beings who want to add value to the world. When someone says they have no purpose or don't know what their purpose is, they are often referring to one big accomplishment that makes their mark on the world. In short, we want to matter.

The Merriam-Webster dictionary defines purpose as "the feeling of being determined to do or achieve something; the aim or goal of a person: what a person is trying to do or become." Pay attention to that last part of the definition; purpose is what a person is *trying to become.*

One of my favorite books is *The Purpose Driven Life* by Rick Warren. He wrote a line that completely reset my definition of finding my purpose: "Your purpose is to make God smile." When I read that simple statement, I felt as though a huge boulder had been lifted from my shoulders. Just make God smile. Wow! I didn't have to be Mother Teresa or Gandhi. I didn't have to swim the English Channel or perform some amazing feat of heroism.

I just had to be the best Cindy I could be and make God smile. This was especially soothing to me because of all the religious condemnation I had experienced.

Isn't it a huge relief to know that you do not have to figure out some world-changing task that only you can accomplish? That said, keep in mind that the clarity work you are doing right now may start to reveal more specific purposes for your life. The next step of answering the question of who you *want* to be will help you find your purpose, because when you become the best person you can be, you will make your mark on the world around you.

Hold everything!

Before you move on, do the work! Take the time to write your thoughts about who you are in the five different areas discussed in this chapter. The importance of this first step cannot be emphasized enough. It is the key to figuring out your life. It is your foundation. It may sound like a lot of work, but in my coaching office, I help my clients do a "mind dump" onto a whiteboard, and this whole section usually only takes an hour. Please see Resources page 167 for more information on how to do a mind dump.

PROGRESS CHECK

Let's take a moment to check in before proceeding. First, did you complete the exercises up to this point? If you did, you should now have clarity on *who you are* right now in your Spiritual, Physical, Mental, and Emotional states, and in your Relationships.

Who You Want to Be

Now that you have gotten clarity in these five areas of who you are now, let's explore them again to see what changes you want to make to become the person you want to be.

When you review your answers on the worksheet, you may notice that you have some traits that don't quite fit the person you want to be. It takes brutal honesty to see ourselves clearly. Are you the best person you can be? It is my experience that no one believes they are the best they can possibly be. We are all a work in progress. Don't beat yourself up; let's just figure out what you want to change about yourself in each of the areas.

Making life-changing decisions can cause your Mr. Prickly to start shouting at you, "You can't change that! What would people think? It's just who you are! This is too much work!"

Just tell him to stifle all that for now. Remember, you control your thoughts. Put aside any guilty feelings or doubts, and keep focused. We will deal with all the emotions later.

Now let's revisit the five areas of your life from a different perspective—Who You Want To Be.

SPIRITUAL

If the religion or teachings you were taught in the past no longer ring true for you now, you may decide you want to fulfill your spiritual needs in another way. What beliefs aren't in harmony with your actions? Does another form of worship fit better?

Would volunteering for a cause that touches you deeply fulfill a spiritual need? What do you feel is missing? Would meditation fill a spiritual need? Write down the changes you want to make to fill your spirit. Don't worry about how to make the changes yet or who might be upset with you for changing. Just be true to you.

_____

_____

_____

_____

_____

_____

_____

PHYSICAL

We can all be judgmental about our bodies. We see little flaws that no one else would ever notice.

Pause for a minute, and go look at yourself in a full-length mirror. Notice what you think about yourself when you look in the mirror. Your attitude affects how you appear to the world: your posture, tone, and degree of confidence. The goal is to go from seeing all your flaws to focusing on how marvelous and magnificent your physical body is.

Your senses allow you to enjoy the taste of foods, the sight of the beauty of nature, the sounds of music and laughter, the touch of different textures, and the smells of fragrance. In addition to these five basic senses, all of your internal organs function without your giving them a second thought. All of your muscles support and move you without your conscious awareness. Can you appreciate that these processes are continually happening inside your body?

If you don't accept your body as it is right now, it is important that you learn to see it in a different light. Consider what you want to change about your physical body, then write down your answers to the following three questions. (See the example answers that follow.)

Who I am today:_____

Who I want to be:_____

What I really want:_____

Example answers:

> Who I am today: twenty pounds overweight; high blood pressure

> Who I want to be: confident in a bathing suit; not fixated on my weight

> What I really want: join a gym; request an eating plan from my doctor

MENTAL

Your thoughts have a lot to do with how you feel, how you are doing in your life, and all other aspects of your overall well-being.

Who do you want to be in your thoughts? If someone were to describe you, would they say you were a half-full or half-empty type of person? Are you positive or negative most of the time? Are you happy or a complainer? Do you take advantage of all your mental capabilities? Are you frustrated because you know you are capable of more? Consider the way you spend your time. You may have addictions that are making you unhappy; in fact, they may be harming you. Could boredom be causing these harmful behaviors?

Bernie came to my office with a gambling addiction. At thirty years old, he had already lost over $300,000. His wife, friends, and family were at their breaking points with him because he had started and stopped gambling many times over the last nine years. When he came to see me, he said he had to stop because he was now losing everything, including his relationships.

I asked Bernie what made him start gambling. He said he did not know. When he began to tell me about his life, I could see that he was highly intelligent, but everything had been given to him. His parents had provided well for him throughout his childhood, and he now worked in his father's store. He even had an arranged marriage. There were no challenges in his life, no excitement.

I asked him what he had accomplished so far. He did not know. I asked him what he did for fun. He said "Gamble." I asked him if it was possible that he was bored and used gambling as a way of filling a void. His eyes lit up. "Yes," he said, "I have been very bored!"

I explained to Bernie that people who are intelligent and do not give their brains enough stimulation will form habits that give their brains some form of activity to fill the time and create a sense of accomplishment. He said, "You are right! I am smart, and I haven't been utilizing my intelligence. I've just been coasting along. I haven't been challenging myself or accomplishing anything, so every time I try to give up gambling, I get depressed and start all over again."

Bernie had been attending Gamblers Anonymous. After this epiphany, he couldn't wait to tell his peers that he had learned the *why* that was behind his habit. I worked with him to figure out what beneficial activities he could do to give his brain positive activity to acquire what he really desired from life. Creating that plan has now given him purpose. He was able to give up gambling and he fills his time with working toward his dreams.

Think about your habits and activities. Do you think they are beneficial to you and others? Or are they just time fillers? Could it be that you are bored? If you are unhappy, depressed, or anxious, think about how much of these feelings are mental and how much are emotional. Write down the habits and activities you would like to change.

_____

_____

_____

_____

_____

_____

_____

_____

EMOTIONAL

We all want balance, focus, and contentment in our lives. You, too, can have these when the emotions that support your stability become part of who you are instead of merely fleeting moments.

In Worksheet 4, you have been filling out detailed answers to who you are and who you want to be. For example, if you have an easily triggered temper, you might write down "calm" in the *Who You Want to Be* column. If you are highly emotional right now, the change you want to make might be "peaceful."

You may be thinking, "What if my partner/boss/children are the source of the problems? What if I am being emotionally abused? How do I make the abuser change? If they would change, everything would be fine. I can't be balanced when I'm in this situation. I only fight back to protect myself." If this is your situation, please read on. (If it is not your situation, and you take 100 percent responsibility for your emotions, skip to the next section, Relationships.)

First, let me give you a hug. It is heart-wrenching to be in an abusive relationship. You are not alone. Since one in two marriages end in divorce, there are a lot of hurting people out there, and not many relationships end peacefully. When I was in an abusive marriage, I tried everything. I tried being nice. I tried fighting back. I tried praying. I tried going to counselling. At one point, I attended Al Anon meetings, for families of alcoholics. One of the first things I heard at my first meeting made me extremely angry. I was told that I could only change myself. *Really? I'm not the problem!* I thought. I remember leaving that meeting feeling even more hopeless. I cried the entire way home. Those words rang in my ears for the next week. How was I supposed to change myself and in turn make him stop drinking and verbally abusing me?

Since I felt desperate for help, I kept going to the meetings. After my third visit, I started to understand what they were saying. I had the power to change my emotional response to whatever was happening in my life. But I still didn't know how.

At the same time, I saw an Oprah show that featured Patricia Evans, the author of *The Verbally Abusive Relationship*. As she described a typical abusive conversation, I literally dropped the laundry basket I had been holding and sat down to take in every word. I was not crazy! She was describing my relationship exactly. I ran out to the bookstore and bought the book that afternoon. I devoured every word.

I finally understood what I needed to change. I realized that I did have a choice regarding how I react. I didn't have to become abusive in return. I didn't have to stay in the relationship. Reading that book gave me back my power to make decisions for my life.

Every time someone says or does something to you, you *do* have a choice about how you will react. When you hear yourself saying, "They *make me* . . .," alarm bells should go off, because no one can *make* you react in a specific way. You are choosing your reaction. Knowing who you are will give you the emotional grounding to be true to yourself when you respond. Will the other person change? You never know. You have no control over that situation, but if you stay true to who you want to be and listen to your gut, you will make the right decisions. You can have emotional stability and calm among the chaos. This clarity work will be your emotional foundation.

Even though it may not seem like progress yet, you are already moving forward. With each turn of the page, with each worksheet you complete, and with each entry in your *My Book of* _____*(your name)*_____, you are one step closer to gaining control.

RELATIONSHIPS

Review the list of people you made in Worksheet 2. Then think about who you want to be in relation to the people in your life and your attitude toward them. You also need to figure out what you want to change about yourself to improve the quality of your relationships.

Again, writing the answers on paper is extremely important because it will help your brain to shift from emotion to logic. Go back to the worksheet now, and look at the relationships you gave a low rating number to. Then take three deep breaths, and write down the changes you could make to improve the quality of each of those relationships so that they would change to a higher rating number that would make you happier.

This exercise can be hard because you might feel like the other person should be the one to change. Or you may feel anger, grief, or sadness within that relationship. Stepping aside from those emotions to see how you could change the dynamic by your own actions is difficult. If you do have difficulty with that, ask yourself what emotions you are feeling. Close your eyes and really zero in on words to describe what you feel. Write them down. Once you identify them, write down the opposite word.

For example:

> Relationship: Mother (rating #2 out of 10) What I feel to make my relationship a #2: anger, resentment, hurt.
>
> Opposite Words: calm, forgiveness, heal.

Keeping in mind that this exercise is to benefit you, can you set aside emotion to be more logical to get to the feelings you really want in that relationship?

If you can't move past your feelings, how long do you need to feel anger, grief or sadness? It may seem ridiculous to set a time period for these feelings, but try it for two reasons. Giving yourself permission to be upset is calming. It validates your feelings. Giving yourself a time frame programs your brain to realize that there will be an end to these emotions and a beginning to feeling better. If you need a few hours, a day or two to hide under the covers, pound a pillow, or pour out your problems to someone who will listen, know that this behavior is okay. Literally set an alarm clock to go off at the end of your allowed time. When the alarm rings, sit down and complete the rest of this chapter.

(Note: If you are grieving a current loss, please skip to Chapter 9 now, and return here after you have completed it.)

What You Want

What you want is different from the section you just completed about *who you want to be*. Who you want to be is about you making internal changes to your individual soul, your inner being, and who the world sees. *What you want* is about how to make those changes happen by changing exterior circumstances.

Take a moment to go back and look at what you wrote about the changes you want to make. Then ask yourself the following questions for each change. Fill out Worksheet 4 to help you get clear on what you want to change. See Worksheet 5 as an example of how to fill out the worksheet.

- ☞ Why do I want to make this change?

- ☞ How will it change my life or the lives of those around me for the better?

- ☞ What do I need to make this happen?

- ☞ Where can I get help?

- ☞ Who can help me?

Keep asking the questions until you have a clear picture of how you can make the changes in each of the five areas so you can become the best version of you. Once you have finished the work, you will be ready to learn the key to make your wishes happen!

Worksheet 4. Gain Clarity

CLARITY		
WHO I AM	WHO I WANT TO BE	WHAT I WANT
Spiritual:		
Physical:		
Mental:		
Emotional:		
Relationships:		
People:		
Places:		
Possessions:		
Prosperity:		
Purpose:		

Worksheet 5 is an example to help you fill out Worksheet 4.

Worksheet 5. Gain Clarity Example

CLARITY		
WHO I AM	WHO I WANT TO BE	WHAT I WANT
Spiritual: Lost; Broken	Peaceful; Confident	Share common beliefs with others; Search for church
Physical: Overweight; high blood pressure	Healthy; Attractive; Energetic	Meal plan; Cooking lessons
Mental: Confused; Unfocused; Bored	Happy; Clear; Purposeful; Educated	Grief recovery, meditation; Finish college degree
Emotional: Sad; Angry	Content; Peaceful	Stop crying; Have more fun
Relationships:		
People: Lonely	Someone people like	More friends
Places: Solitary	Fun to be around	Hobbies/Activities I like
Possessions: Selfish	Giving; Charitable	Volunteer with causes
Prosperity: Broke	Not worried about money	Build savings; Pay off loan
Purpose: None	Content; Sure; Have meaning	To matter to someone

CHAPTER 2

Commitment

Most people fail not because of lack of desire,
but because of lack of commitment.

—VINCE LOMBARDI

You read in the Quick Start section how the Romans thought we had a main vein that went from the ring finger directly to the heart, which they called the love vein. This is the finger that represents the second of the 5C's: Commitment.

Commitments are set in stone by public declaration, such as when a couple gets married. The couple stands before an officiant and declares their love for one another in a ceremony, with friends and family gathered to witness their declaration of intent to be loyal to each other for the rest of their lives. Rings are exchanged as a symbol of that pledge. Wearing wedding rings is an outward symbol to any onlooker of the couple's marital commitment.

Ceremony + Symbol = Commitment

How committed are you to getting what you want? Are you sure? If you are committed, why don't you have it already? How many times have you heard someone say they want to lose weight while they were consuming a hot fudge sundae? Are they really committed? No. They are saying it out loud because they think they should lose weight, but they really don't want to.

Whatever you say after the word "but" is a justification of why you don't really believe what you just said. For instance, "I want to lose weight, but it is just so hard with my schedule." Translation: "I don't want to change my eating habits, exercise, adjust my schedule," and so on.

Why not have a commitment ceremony and declare to your friends and loved ones your commitment to lose weight, write a book, get a better job, or whatever you view as your personal goal? This keeps you accountable, because people will be asking how you are doing with your goal.

When I had the idea for my first book, *Moving Past the Death of a Loved One*, I told a few people about my plan. At first, saying it out loud was uncomfortable. This feeling matched my insecurity about whether I could write the book. I had only started writing down a skeleton of ideas, but telling someone helped me to keep working on the project.   Every time they saw me or we talked on the phone, they would ask how the book was coming along. Just talking about it reignited my passion and helped me push through any doubts.

As my confidence grew, the book took shape. There were times when I wanted to quit because Mr. Prickly was whispering things like, "Who are you to write a book? What if no one wants to read the book? This is hard. Why not just take it easy for a while and write later?" I would then go to a networking event or a family function, and people would ask how the book was coming along. I knew I had to keep working, because I didn't want to tell them I wasn't making progress. Even though writing the book took longer than I had anticipated, and longer than most people thought it would, the day I sent my final edit to the publisher was a day to celebrate.

Of course, when I started writing this book, the whole process repeated itself. It's human to doubt ourselves, even when we have done something similar before.

Commitment is the key to making things happen. It is the difference between a weekend warrior and an Olympic athlete. Who do you think is more committed to their sport? Olympic athletes are so committed that every decision made is in alignment with their ultimate goal. Everything they do, eat, practice, and plan is in harmony with the goal of winning a gold medal. They declare this commitment by being on the team and representing their country. Even though their chances of winning the gold are slim, they do not allow such a thought to discourage them.

When you are not committed to a positive outcome, you can experience prolonged grief, depression, and a spiral of negative events that will make the situation worse. No matter what the plan for moving past your current situation, you must make a commitment and pledge to yourself to stay the course.

When was the last time you totally committed to getting what you wanted and then got it? Think about what made the difference and apply that level of intensity to your new goals. Look at your list of changes you want to make. Prioritize them by first doing the one that will make the most positive difference in your life.

You must believe that you are smart enough, capable enough, and resourceful enough to go beyond this temporary bump in the road of life. Keep telling yourself that this situation is not your fault. Bad things happen to everyone. We all do the best we can in the situation. This is another opportunity to learn new life lessons that will continue to make you stronger and more empathetic to others in the future. Commit to remaining positive and seeking a support system to help you through.

Consider wearing a ring as a symbol of commitment to remind yourself that you know in your heart things will get better or that you will reach your goals. Every time you feel hopeless, fearful, or discouraged, look at the ring. Feel the connection to your heart, say a prayer to someone higher than yourself (if that is your belief), and ask for strength. Close your eyes, make a fist as you feel renewed strength, and envision grabbing your future. Smile. Open your eyes and continue with your day.

Find a cheerleader to whom you can declare your commitment for each change. Look for someone whose opinion you respect. Do not choose someone who will nag you or make passive-aggressive comments (you know who these people are). If you can't think of anyone near to you, think outside your immediate circle. Do you have a former classmate, teacher, workmate, or second cousin whom you trust and who has always proven themselves as an advocate? If not, consider joining a group that has similar interests or goals, such as a mastermind group, a networking group, or a yoga class, where you can meet friendly people. Tell someone in the group what you are trying to change. The simple act of telling someone else will make your goal real. When you allow the universe to hear you say it out loud, and you follow the path in the direction of your dreams, you will be surprised at how things will fall into place.

If you are like me, your inner voice is probably going crazy right now with a laundry list of reasons why this won't work. In the next chapter, you will learn now to tame your Mr. Prickly by overcoming your challenges.

CHAPTER 3

Challenges

There are no great men, only great challenges that ordinary men are forced by circumstances to meet.

—WILLIAM FREDERICK HALSEY, JR.

At this point you have gotten clarity and have committed to moving forward. Have you ever noticed that it seems as soon as you commit and start to move forward beyond your initial declaration, life will inevitably throw you the middle finger? Yes, challenges will occur. Things will not always go smoothly. Even well-thought-out plans will not work out all the time. It's not a coincidence that the third finger represents the third step in the 5C's: Challenges.

Being prepared for what could go wrong will help you remain focused and ready for whatever comes. It is called a backup plan. Athletes prepare for hurdles, what-ifs, and roadblocks. They think ahead about defense against the opposing team's offense, what they will do if the weather is bad, or if a team member is injured. When planning a road trip, travelers prepare for car trouble, detours, and where to stop to rest. Pilots practice for engine trouble, emergency landings, and storms.

You are like a long-distance runner, a traveler through time, and the pilot of your own life. Begin thinking of things that could go wrong and how you would deal with them if and when they happen. Preparation is the first key to staying the course and progressing faster toward your goal. When an obstacle pops up, you can smile and knowingly say, "I knew you'd show your ugly head, but you can't beat me. I'm prepared to conquer you head on!"

Share your plan with friends and family. They may laugh. They may think you will never succeed. Their discouragement may be your biggest challenge to overcome. It can also be your greatest motivation. However, sharing your vision with others will begin to bring resources into your life that will propel you faster and faster toward your goal. When I start sharing my dreams, I am amazed at how someone will appear who is the perfect person to teach me the next step.

As you move through your plan, you will find that there are two types of challenges: external and internal. Let's look at each one.

External Challenges

External challenges can be circumstances, lack of knowledge, or other people. Let's say you want to buy a house, but you don't have enough money. This is a challenge. How will you handle it? Will you analyze your budget to determine where you can cut back? Is there a part-time job you could obtain to make more money? There is a solution if you are willing to think of all the possibilities.

People who discourage you can be an external challenge, especially if they are your significant other. What will you do when they say something hurtful? Will you allow them to squash your dreams, or will you rise to the challenge and find a way through?

What if you want to start a business but have no experience? Are there classes you can take to learn how? Do you know someone who is a business owner who could mentor you?

There is an answer for every challenge. You simply must use your imagination, be committed to finding an answer, and then follow through.

Internal Challenges

What is your biggest internal challenge? If you are like most people, your biggest obstacle is fear. Your internal dialogue, your Mr. Prickly, will pull out all of your fearful thoughts and throw them at you. This is your defense system trying to protect you from harm. It's a good thing that we have this ability so we don't do things that can put us in danger. Most of us these days have the essential elements of life, such as food, clothing, and shelter, so this voice has turned into a critical and negative force whenever we wish to try something new or different.

Did you give your negative inner voice a name? If you didn't, do it now. Write it down here:

_____

Dealing with Your Mr. Prickly

There are specific ways you can deal with your Mr. Prickly instead of just trying to ignore him, which may be difficult if not impossible. For example:

1. Listen to him just enough to understand which fear is stopping you.

2. Write down his comments.

3. Next to each comment, write down how you will overcome that fear.

4. Ask yourself:

   ☞   Is this fear real?

   ☞   Where is this fear coming from?

   ☞   What is my strategy to overcome this fear?

Most of the time we fear the unknown. Because the future is unknown, we could live in fear all the time. When you filled out Worksheet 4 under *Who I Want to Be*, you probably did not write, "I want to live in fear all of the time." Go back to that worksheet, review your answers under *Who I Am* and *Who I Want to Be*, and notice what your Mr. Prickly is saying to you.

Let's look at Marsha, who wants to be healthier. She writes down specific details on who and what she wants to be.

Who am I? *Twenty pounds overweight*

Who do I want to be? *Attractive, confident*

What do I really want? *To be healthy*

Commitment: *I declared my commitment to my doctor.*

Challenges

External: *My schedule, my love of fried foods, social drinking*

Internal: *Not wanting to get out of bed early to exercise*

Mr. Prickly says, "But it feels so good in bed. You don't have to go to the gym today. Sleep in. Go tomorrow."

Fill in your challenges on Worksheet 6. Writing down what your Mr. Prickly says will make it easier for you to address the fears, and you will have a visual reminder.

Worksheet 6: Challenges

MY CHALLENGES	MR. PRICKLY STATEMENTS: WHY I CAN'T DO IT
Spiritual:	
Physical:	
Mental:	
Emotional:	
Relationships:	
Financial:	

Don't worry about how you are going to rise to your challenges yet. In the next chapter, you will discover how to overcome both external and internal challenges by creating a plan.

CHAPTER 4

Creation

Our goals can only be reached through a vehicle
of a plan ... There is no other route to success.

—PABLO PICASSO

Whatever you want to accomplish, whether it be in business or in your personal life, creation of a plan is like putting an address in a GPS. The directions become clear because you know where you want to go. Your pointer finger represents the fourth of the 5C's: Creation of a plan. It reminds you that you are moving forward toward those goals.

At this point, you have gotten clarity, you have committed, and your challenges have been acknowledged. Now you will figure out the steps you need to get what you want.

X_____**X**
TODAY   **GOAL**

Review your answers in Worksheet 4 under *What I Want*. Did you prioritize them and choose the one that will be most immediately beneficial? Let's create a road map to get there. This process is what I refer to as your PGS—your Personal Guidance System.

We often want to just leap from today to the goal, but obtaining change does not work that way. There are action steps you will take in between that will move you closer.

For example, while writing my first book, one of my action steps was to meet Jack Canfield, the co-author of *Chicken Soup for the Soul*. Who better to get book advice from than someone who has more than 500 million books in distribution? I knew he was the expert from whom I wanted to learn. But how? I didn't know how I would meet him when I wrote down that step. However, because I had put the idea out there, when I got to that point in my timeline, I did research on how I could meet him.

I discovered he was going to speak at a conference I was planning to attend, and I shared this news with my husband. He laughed and said, "There will be hundreds of women there who will want to meet him. You'll be lucky if you're able to even get close to him." For the next few months I kept reading my written goal, "I will meet Jack Canfield and speak to him one-on-one."

On the second day of the conference I was waiting for the elevator in the lobby of the hotel when I noticed a small crowd of excited women gathered at the front door. I wasn't sure what was happening, but as the crowd parted, I saw Jack Canfield. He had just arrived, and the bellboy was bringing his luggage to the elevator. Mr. Canfield signed a few autographs and then excused himself to get settled. As he approached the elevator, the door opened, and we both stepped in.

The bellboy said, "You must be famous. Who are you?" Mr. Canfield humbly said, "I'm an author of a book series." The kid shrugged his shoulders and looked away, having no idea he had just spoken with the co-founder of the billion-dollar empire based on his *Chicken Soup* books. I, on the other hand, could not believe that I was one-on-one with Jack Canfield in the privacy of an elevator.

I told him how I had written down my goal of meeting him and having a one-on-one conversation with him. He smiled and said, "Then it isn't a coincidence that we met," and he put out his hand to shake mine. I introduced myself as Cindy Cipriani, the author of *Moving Past the Death of a Loved One* (the book I was writing at the time). When the elevator stopped, we both got out. He said it was nice to meet me and that he looked forward to speaking with me at the conference. As we began walking down the hall, he gave me a curious look. I said, "Oh, I'm not stalking you. My room is on this floor, too!" He laughed, and we parted ways.

The following day I spoke with him again and took a photograph. He had kind words of wisdom about never giving up and said if I ever needed anything, to ask. Wow! I couldn't wait to call my husband and tell him that my written goal had come true. Since then I have had many conversations with him where he has given me invaluable advice, and he has graciously endorsed this book.

You never know who you will meet who can help you. Maybe the person sitting next to you on a bus is just the person to introduce you to your next boss. Perhaps a friend of a friend is in the publishing business and can help you publish your book. Perhaps a coworker knows someone who just went through a similar crisis and can give you the right advice and a needed ear to listen. If you do not tell people what you want and need, you will be sitting by yourself on an island, wondering why you feel so alone.

Creation of Your Plan

Now that you have gotten clarity, committed and identified your challenges, you are ready to create a plan to conquer them.

Let's use Marsha's example at the end of the last chapter to create a plan to conquer her challenges. Marsha writes more details about her challenges.

> **My external challenge:** My friend Jane is always sabotaging my diet.
>
> **Creation of a plan to conquer this challenge:** I will conquer this by politely telling her of my commitment and by ordering healthy foods when I am with her, even if she pressures me to try less-healthy choices.
>
> **My internal challenge:** Not wanting to get out of bed early. I know Mr. Prickly will say, "But it feels so good in bed. You don't have to go to the gym today. Sleep in. Go tomorrow."
>
> **Creation of a plan to conquer this challenge:** To overcome Mr. Prickly, I will place two alarms on the other side of the bedroom, making it necessary to get up to turn them off. I commit to staying up once the alarms are shut off.

To create your plan, review the challenges you wrote down in each of the five areas in Worksheet 6. Next, write a detailed step-by-step plan of how to move closer to your goal by overcoming your roadblocks.

Once you have written your plan, you are ready to put it into motion. Every morning when you get up, point your finger forward as a reminder that today you are getting one step closer to your dreams, then reread your action steps. Visualize yourself achieving one more step toward your goal.

There is still one more "C" to implement as you roll down the path toward your final goal. It is the key to staying the course and not giving up.

CHAPTER 5

Celebrate!

Remember to celebrate milestones as
you prepare for the road ahead.

—NELSON MANDELA

The last "C" of the 5C's is as important as every other step—maybe even more so. Celebrating your successes on your way to your goal is absolutely crucial in continuing to move forward. Every New Year's Eve millions of people make resolutions, but just a few weeks later, they give up. I believe this is because they haven't acknowledged any progress along the way. They may have made a few steps to change, but as time moves forward and they haven't achieved their ultimate goal, the work of change becomes too difficult and boring.

Every time you gain clarity about what you want, commit to achieving it, prepare for the challenges, and create a plan, give yourself a thumbs up! This gesture represents celebration and accomplishment.

We often make the mistake of thinking we need to accomplish our final goal before we can celebrate a success. Recognizing and commemorating each step along the way will help maintain your momentum. It's like telling a teenager that they can go to the movies after they clean their room. They don't want to do it, but once they do and are rewarded, they see that it wasn't so bad.

Change is hard. If you reward yourself along the way to your goal, your brain will say, "I didn't want to do that step, but it wasn't so bad because I got to celebrate! Now let's do the next step so I can celebrate again!"

We can sometimes feel guilty rewarding ourselves, or we make light of our accomplishments and tell ourselves they are not a big deal. If you can't get excited about your achievements, who will? Make a list of little (and big) things you can do to reward yourself—celebrations you can enjoy for each step of the path—and make sure you do them. Treat yourself to a bubble bath. Have lunch with a friend.

You can keep your reward as a fun secret that only you are aware of, or you can share it and celebrate with someone who will be thrilled for you. Either way, don't take life so seriously that you forget to laugh and enjoy.

My husband and I own a residential remodeling company, and I was a designer with the business for seventeen years. Whenever a client chose my design, I celebrated by going next door to the convenience store to buy a single chocolate-covered cherry. It was a little indulgence that only I knew about. Chocolate-covered cherries are my favorite candy, so I would save getting one for these celebrations. It was my way of saying, "Good job!"

You don't have to reward yourself with candy or food. You can also celebrate by taking a walk, sitting by a body of water and relaxing, getting a massage, having friends over to watch your favorite movie, calling a friend to share your accomplishment, ringing a bell, and so on. Make a list of things that bring you joy, and do one each time you take a step closer to your goal. Not only will you be making progress, but you will be living your life with celebration, which is the ultimate goal.

If you can't think of ways to celebrate, here is a suggestion. One of the first things I coach my clients to do is to make a "Fun List." When you are in a state of confusion, depression, and chaos, it can be hard to think of fun things you enjoy. In fact, many of my clients say that this is one of the hardest exercises they do because they have stopped enjoying themselves due to their problems and stresses.

To make this easier, keep a small tablet next to your bed, and each night before you go to sleep, write down three things that you loved doing that day, three things that made you smile and had fun doing. I call this my "Today I Loved____Book." They can be little things like the feel of flannel sheets on a cold night, playing with your dog, or watching a sunset. I have been doing this for years, and this has become like a diary. I can look back and see exactly what I was doing on any given day. When I need a way to celebrate, I look at my lists and pick something that brought me joy.

Making this list serves several purposes. Part of achieving clarity is changing your thought patterns. Worry is meditating on the negative. Getting your mind to remember positive and fun activities will steer your thoughts away from worry and the current problems. It will remind you that you can have enjoyment and that better times are just around the corner.

Another added benefit is that when you think about your day right before you go to bed, especially when you focus on the positive, your brain gets to file away the things that happened that day so you can sleep better.

As adults, we sometimes forget that life should be enjoyed. We stop playing just for the pleasure of it. When was the last time you swung on a swing, skipped down the street, rode a bike around the block (not to train for a race in skintight spandex but to feel the breeze on your face), colored with crayons, or watched television in your pajamas on a Saturday morning? All these activities can be on your Fun List, and you can pick one to do after each step toward your ultimate accomplishment. Once you begin this list, your mind will automatically start reminding you of small things you enjoy doing that you have not done in a long while.

Another great way to remind yourself to add to your list is to make a vision board filled with photographs of things you love. Get a large poster board and a bunch of magazines (or look online and print some out). Sit down with a glue stick and scissors. Start looking closely at all the photographs. Do you see something that makes you smile? Cut it out to add to your vision board.

Add photographs as you think of more and more things that make you happy. Take items on your vision board and turn them into fun things to do to celebrate. For instance, I have a photograph of a horse on my board because I love horses. Items on my Fun List are to go horseback riding or drive to a horse farm near me and just sit and watch the horses. Another photograph is of flowers. In the dead of winter, I like to treat myself to one single flower to brighten my desk and remind myself of an accomplishment, or simply that I am special to myself.

Next to your list of clear action steps, write a celebration that you will do after each accomplishment!

There you have it: Clarity, Commitment, Challenges, Creation of a plan, and Celebrate! Use The 5C Solution to go from confusion to clarity to get out of a crisis, to rise to any challenge, and to establish a solid foundation of who you are, who you want to be, and what you want in life. You always have your hand with you, so you can use this tool at any time. Show your friends, co-workers, and family how to walk through these simple steps confidently to figure out any problem, accomplish any mission, and work toward any goal.

PART II

Practical Applications of the 5C's

CHAPTER 6

The 5C Solution
for Everyday Life

The 5C Solution is fantastic for use in your everyday life, and if you teach the 5C's strategy to those you work with, family members, classmates, and others, you will all begin speaking the 5C's language. The great thing about The 5C Solution is that your left hand is your tool to remember, so you always have instant access to remind you how to go from confused to celebration in a matter of seconds. (If you don't have a left hand, use your right hand or even just a picture of a hand.)

Let's take a look at how The 5C Solution can be applied to daily life in the areas of health and wellness.

When a client says, "I got clear that I need to lose weight. I am committed to diet and exercise, but my challenge is I don't have time, and I love fatty foods. What can I do?" we can create a plan that fits their lifestyle and that they will stick to. For every pound they lose, we plan a celebration that doesn't involve food. Now, this is not a diet book, nor am I a dietician. However, it is fair to say that a large majority of my clients want to change something about their health or weight when they do their clarity work. It is also fair to say that most people know they need to develop healthy habits.

The key to making changes is not that people need more education. How often have you said, "I should eat better," "I should lose weight," "I should quit smoking," or some other "should"? Whenever you say "should," it is because you think other people are thinking it, but you don't want to do it.

The key to making change is to commit. How committed are you to what you say you want? Ask yourself how committed you are to losing weight or exercising. Rate your commitment on a scale of 1 to 10, with 1 being not committed and 10 being deeply committed. If you are below a 9, then you have to get more clarity on *why* this change is important to you, or it just won't happen. You must have a good enough reason to make change for it to happen.

Studies have shown that the number one reason people want to improve their eating habits is to improve their heart health. In fact, 20 percent of consumers list cardiovascular health as their top goal in relation to changing their dietary habits.

People who have been diagnosed with a health-related issue—diabetes, high blood pressure, high cholesterol, heart attack, or other serious condition—take losing weight more seriously than those who don't have obvious health issues. They may have thought about losing weight before the diagnosis but weren't committed enough to making changes until it got real. It just wasn't important enough until they learned that their body was starting to break down. Suddenly, all of the challenges that were in the way before (time, money, love of fast food, etc.) fade to the background. Once they commit to it, change starts to happen. They still have the challenges, but their emphasis is on creating a plan that works.

The same thing happens for any life situation that needs to be changed, whether it is in business, relationships, or personal choices. People hate change, but change is exactly what needs to happen to shift the outcome.

Let's take a look at how The 5C Solution can be applied to daily life in the areas of education and career.

A common issue I see among my clients who are in their fifties and sixties is dissatisfaction with their position in life. Many thought they would be "more successful" or "happy" by the time they reached middle age. They comment on how quickly life has gone by, how they don't feel middle-aged, and how the fear of growing old and not achieving their dreams is weighing on them.

This is when mid-life crises happen. When I was younger, I used to think that the term was just a funny label given to old men who suddenly bought Corvettes and traded in their wives for younger women. In reality, it hits everyone in one way or another. At mid-life, we start to question who we are, especially if we haven't done our clarity work when we were younger. Time is ticking by, and making the most of it becomes a priority. When we suddenly realize that half of our life or more is over, our youthful body is starting to age and wrinkle, and our doctors are half our age, things start to look different.

You bring great value to your peers, family, and the business community through the experience and wisdom you have accumulated, although you may not yet realize it. You can use The 5C Solution to get clarity on how much you have accomplished and to figure out if you simply need to adjust your attitude or if you need something more to make you feel successful.

When I do the clarity work with my middle-aged clients, they often feel intimidated by younger colleagues who have college degrees. In the 1970s and 1980s, many kids followed a career path after high school instead of going to college. If you feel that an education for personal accomplishment or to further your career would be useful, then you can use The 5C Solution. Get clarity on why this is important to you, give it a rating as to how important it is, how you would feel about yourself if you went back to school, and what a degree would do for you. Think about which subjects you would like to take, and what degree you would like to commit to getting.

You may feel challenged by time, money, and thinking you are too old. Acknowledge this, and then create a plan. You can research schools, classes, tuition, credits for life experience, and schedule talks with college advisors on the best path to a degree. Taking this first step of contemplating this action is cause for celebration, so remember to stop and reward yourself for looking into higher education.

Once you have all your information, use The 5C Solution again. This time, narrow down whether you will move forward or not by getting clarity on the exact degree you want. Commit by choosing a school and telling someone close to you about your goal to get a degree. What challenges might stop you? Write down everything your Mr. Prickly says, such as, "I don't have the money," "This will take too long," or "I'm too old."

It really is never too late to go back to school, and Nola Ochs is a perfect example. Nola received her college diploma on May 14, 2007, when she was ninety-five, also earning her a Guinness World Record as the world's oldest college graduate. She went on to earn her master's degree at the age of ninety-eight.

Now that we have the age objection out of the way, any other concerns you may have will also not stop you from creating a step-by-step plan. Sit down with an advisor, and map out the class strategy. Perhaps you can take online courses as you work. Find out if your current employer has college tuition money available for their employees that you could take advantage of. Think outside the box by talking to others who have completed their degrees later in life.

If you have clarity as to why this is important to you, are committed to making it happen, have listed your challenges and created a plan to overcome them, then all that is left is to start, and celebrate after each class.

Time will pass whether you do something about your dreams or not. The bonus is that staying mentally active is a secret weapon against aging. You are a valuable commodity because of the wisdom you have accumulated during your lifetime from the many experiences, difficulties, and relationships you have had. If you believe otherwise, it is time to gain clarity on the value you bring to your peers, family, and the business community. You are what you believe. Why not get out of your own way and make it happen?

No matter what your age, there are career courses that will

help you get a promotion. Or perhaps you want to learn a new skill set that will enable you to change careers so that you can do something more fulfilling.

Maybe education is not what you desire. Perhaps there are activities you love but haven't taken time to do. If you feel that life is just work, work, work, then use The 5C Solution to gain clarity on what you can do to bring fun and fulfillment into your daily life. Perhaps you always wanted to learn to fly an airplane, volunteer for a cause, or be an artist. Use The 5C Solution to first gain clarity on what you feel is missing, things like fun, relationships, hobbies, being part of a group, spiritual pursuits, and so on. Then commit to the one that would bring you the most joy. Write down all the challenges that may stop you from pursuing your interest, create a plan to overcome them, and celebrate life by enjoying your new activity.

Building a Foundation with The 5C Solution

Life is more complicated than just adding education or activities to your day. Sometimes unexpected crises occur. You can use The 5C Solution to build a solid foundation for all kinds of life situations. The following example demonstrates how to apply the The 5Cs to the challenge of being laid off without warning.

You are called into the boss's office at four o'clock on a Friday afternoon. Out of the blue and with no warning, you are informed that you are being furloughed. As you leave the office, the first thing you feel is shock. Your mind starts racing. *What do I do now? How am I going to pay my bills? This cannot be happening!*

As you walk to your desk and begin packing your personal belongings, the frozen state of shock begins to thaw. A wave of emotions follows. Tears. Anger. *This is not fair! How could they do this to me! I hated this job anyway! I can't wait to get out of here!*

Co-workers want to know what is happening. You explode as you tell them you have just been laid off. None of their sympathy can reach beneath the hurt.

You are embarrassed and confused. Underneath, fear is lurking. How will you tell your family? What about unemployment? How long does it take to collect benefits? A million thoughts run through your head. As soon as you are in your car, you call your spouse. "You aren't going to believe this! I just got laid off! What are we going to do now?"

You drive home, dazed. You wonder what to do first as you walk in the front door. How should you react? Should you be the calm, cool, and collected head of the house so no one panics? Inside, you just want to scream.

You need time to process. You tell your family that things will be fine, thus also reassuring yourself. You give yourself some down time. The adrenaline that was flowing now begins to dissipate, making you feel exhausted. Over the next few days, you feel the beginning of depression. You go through the emotions of grief, because losing your job is a major loss. There are decisions to be made, things to figure out, and changes to take place. For now, you just rest. You set your alarm for a time when you can sit down, start to reason this out, and seek clarity.

USING THE 5C SOLUTION

The previous example describes a very real situation for millions of people. Let's see how using the 5Cs can help, step by step.

Clarity

The first thing to do is to gain clarity. Ask yourself what you need *now*, then write it down. For example, you write:

1. Get information on unemployment.
2. Budget to determine financial situation.
3. Determine which bills must be paid immediately and which ones can wait.
4. Get advice from an accountant or someone who has gone through this.
5. Create a plan to look for another job.

You can help control the emotions and allow yourself time for rational thought when you stop, breathe, and gain clarity.

Commitment

Now that you have gained clarity on what you need, make a commitment to do the work for each of the steps. Tell someone what you are doing so they can help keep you accountable and be a cheerleader along the way.

Challenges

Your Mr. Prickly will certainly raise his ugly head, because you are in a fearful situation. Remember to acknowledge his concerns and thank him for the warnings, but tell him that you got this. Write down all the thoughts that he throws at you so that you can gain clarity on the challenges that may prevent you from moving forward.

Creation of a Plan

Use the action steps you wrote down from gaining clarity to create a step-by-step plan to get them done. For example, you write:

1. Call unemployment office.
2. List current bills, savings, unemployment money coming.
3. Prioritize bills that must be paid first.
4. Note when others are due.
5. Call creditors to ask for delay or cutback on payment until unemployment kicks in.
6. Call for expert advice from accountant or someone who has been laid off before.
7. Make list of places where to look for a new job: LinkedIn, similar companies, web search, friends and family, post on Facebook.
8. Update resume.

Your new job is to find a job. On business days, get up, get dressed, and get out there. Don't allow yourself time to sit around and be depressed because Mr. Prickly will be more than happy to keep you immobile. If you need encouragement, call the friend you committed to and ask him/her to coffee in the morning so you can get pumped up and excited to face new opportunities.

Celebrate!

For each step in your plan, create a fun celebration to do after each step, which will keep you moving toward your goal.

This is The 5C Solution tool in action. You can use this system to figure out any perplexing situation. In fact, you can use The 5C Solution in the moment to decide what you need.

Let's say something comes up and you feel yourself starting to get anxious or agitated. Hold up your left hand and utilize The

5C Solution:

> Clarity: Ask yourself, "What do I really need right now?"
>
> Commit to staying calm and finding an answer.
>
> Challenges: Tell Mr. Prickly that you can handle the situation, then pay attention to his fears so you can.
>
> Create a plan to get what you need in the situation.
>
> Celebrate the outcome.

You may wonder how to do all of this on your own if you don't know how to overcome your challenges. One way is to schedule an appointment with me, either in person or online, and we will figure it out together. Of course, my time is limited, so in order to help more people, I have created an online course, which goes into much more detail than the information in this book does. The step-by-step video modules walk you through how to figure out the most complex, everyday problems in just a few minutes using The 5C Solution. Please see on Resources page 167 for information on this course.

CHAPTER 7

The 5C Solution in Business

As adults, we spend most of our waking hours at work. Whether you own a business or work in one, problems will surface. This is because businesses are made of people, and people have problems. It is rare that a person can leave their personal problems at home and never think about them during the workday, especially with constant access to text messages and social media on their cell phones.

An article by Rescuetime, which makes an app that helps you monitor your time, reported that in 2019, most people checked their phones fifty-eight times a day (with thirty of those during working hours). According to the article, people averaged one minute and fifteen seconds every time they checked their phone, meaning that 37.5 minutes were lost per worker per day. This doesn't take into consideration the distracted thoughts and conversations afterward, when people share with their coworkers. That is a lot of unproductive time!

Business owners debate about banning cell phone use during working hours, but they fear a backlash from employees. After all, people can be just as distracted if they are worried about not having access to what is happening to their friends and loved ones outside of work. How do businesses balance this dynamic?

How does a business owner or manager get the most productivity from their team and provide job satisfaction at the same time? One way is to provide clarity on the importance of each team member's role in the success of the business. Business owners often think they have provided clarity to their team by virtue of their mission statement, yet when asked, most team members can't recite the statement or explain what it truly means to them. When used in the workplace, The 5C Solution is a tool that will bring increased productivity and job satisfaction. Let's consider how this tool can be used by both the owner and the team members.

Business Owners

If you are a business owner, you can use the 5C's to gain clarity for yourself and your employees. Before we start, make sure you have completed the personal work in Part I so you can reflect on who you are, who you want to be, and what you want. Once you have finished it, follow the same steps to analyze your business. If you are a solopreneur, gaining clarity on your own can be difficult. Finding a coach or mentor who can help you answer the following questions will result in greater understanding of how you can be more productive and successful.

Contemplate your answers to the following questions:

> What makes you get up every morning?
> How clear is your vision of your company?
> What are the values your business is built on?
> What is the purpose of your business?

Is your business just a means to make money, or does it serve a greater purpose?

Do you have a written plan for the next year, five years, and ten years? If so, congratulations! You can skip to the *Team* section. If not, you have some work to do.

Let's get started.

In this section, you will review the five areas of clarity you learned about in chapter 3 and apply them to your business. To gain clarity about your business, consider the following questions under each area. Write down your answers on a piece of paper for use later

SPIRITUAL

What is the spirit of your business? What qualities does it reflect? How would someone else describe your business?

If you don't know how your business is viewed, consider sending a survey to past customers, business associates, and vendors to discover the good, the bad, and the ugly so you can get clarity and address these issues. Do an online search for your business, and see what comes up. Many business owners have horrible reviews online and don't even know about them. Don't fool yourself. If business is not as good as you want, there is a reason. If you don't know what it is, you can't fix it.

Does your business serve a larger purpose? If not, is there a charitable organization you can sponsor? How do you support your town and help other business owners? Do you treat others the way you wish to be treated?

PHYSICAL

What is the current physical state of your business? This includes location, building, equipment, tools, and everything you need to run the business efficiently. Do an honest inventory. Ask someone who has never been to your business to come and walk through it. Ask them to say aloud all that they are thinking and observing. Business owners can be blind to what others see clearly.

MENTAL

What is your attitude toward your business? Do you devote time to thinking about how to improve it daily? How much stress does your business put on your personal life? Does the business occupy most of your time and thoughts to the point where you never truly rest? Do you need help or advice on how to grow or how to solve problems? Do you have a good support team, or do you feel alone when making weighty decisions? Does your business fill you with purpose?

EMOTIONAL

What emotions do you feel when you think about work? Are you proud and excited? Depressed and stressed? Are you committed or disengaged? Look at those inside your company. Does your team reflect your emotions?

RELATIONSHIPS

Analyze your relationship with each person in your business. Measure their contributions and personal engagement on a scale of one to ten. Are you cultivating the kinds of relationships you want within the business? Are you contributing to your community?

Think about your customers. Do you have good relationships with them? Do they return to do business with you time and again? Do they refer friends and family to you? Do you know your best clients by name when they walk in the door or if you see them elsewhere? Compare your answers to your personal clarity work.

Business owners have an additional component requiring clarity— the financial picture of their business.

FINANCIAL

Take a hard look at your time/money ratio. Do you have a financial plan in place for the business? Do you plan for the future and for emergencies in the event of a crisis? Are all your legal matters in order? Is your business supplying you with the wealth you desire to fulfill the lifestyle dreams for you and your family? Do you take time off to enjoy the fruits of your labor?

Your written answers to these questions will provide clarity in areas that are working and areas that need changing. When you invest the time to answer these questions, you will be able to apply the 5C's to address the problems you identified. The next step is to commit to taking the time needed to do this work.

There is so much to do every day as an owner that one of the challenges is stepping back and working on the bigger picture. Schedule one day per quarter to go offsite and focus on your business plan, examine what is working and what is not, make a list of the challenges you face, and consult with experts in the creation of a plan to make the necessary changes and improvements. This overview will create greater profitability and provide a roadmap for your team to follow that will lead to celebration.

Team Members

Companies spend time and money on vision statements or mission statements that hang on nice signs in their lobbies, but does anyone really care? Employee engagement starts with living your values and appreciating those who are on your team. As a business owner, you can teach the steps you learned in the last section to your team.

Even though business is about making money, money is made by people. If you have figured out through your own clarity work that you want your company to be more than a place where people come to work to make money, then providing an opportunity for those within the organization to explore their own solutions to life problems will create not only more productivity but also satisfaction and loyalty in your team.

The 5C Solution teaches each team member two things: their role in the organization and their goals for personal prosperity. Business owners and executives know the value of having coaches. What about your team? Imagine the effect of having each person on the team discover who they are, who they want to be, what they really want, and realizing that their job is the means to fulfill their personal goals. Or they may discover they want more. They may need more education, a higher paying position, or a different position altogether in order to be happier.

This may seem scary to the business owner. What if everyone figures out that they are unhappy and want to leave? Relax. That won't happen. Instead, you have created an opportunity to have open dialogue with those who are wishing for more. This communication will open the way for them to take steps that can lead to a promotion, or, if they choose to move on, you will know you contributed to their well-being and future happiness.

Consider the 5C's at work in the following example:

A construction company was divided into three segments: sales, production, and office management. These three teams had different responsibilities, but they all relied on each other. The office staff needed to make appointments for sales. Sales had to be closing for production to have jobs available. Production needed to produce to acquire revenue to pay for office staff. Although they depended on each other, each team did not understand the stresses of the others. Production thought sales made too much money. Sales thought production took too long to do their work. The office management team heard complaints from the other two teams, making them feel as though everyone was unhappy.

The company had team meetings with each group and whole-company meetings to discuss projections, goals, and problem solving. Participation in these meetings was dismal. No one wanted to speak up. Instead, after the meeting, employees would gather around for a "dumpster meeting" in the parking lot, where the production team would stand around the dumpster and say how lame the meeting was, how things would never change, and that the management gave preferential treatment to the sales team. The sales team would meet and complain about how management gave preferential treatment to production.

This went on and on for years. When The 5C Solution was introduced, most of the team wondered what difference it would make. However, when each person started working on their own individual 5C Solution, figuring out exactly what they wanted and how they could contribute to the solutions, magic started happening within the company.

Key management roles were defined. The direction of the business was clarified by the boss, and each person started to see their vital role in the company and its reputation. One older carpenter voiced his interest in a desk job, since it was getting harder to do the physical labor. An office member who did estimating determined that it was time to retire, which opened his position to the older worker, who interviewed and was given the position.

A young apprentice spoke up and asked how he could obtain a promotion. Since the carpenter job was now vacant, the young apprentice received a promotion to a project manager. Then one of the helpers was promoted to apprentice. Morale improved, and everyone became energized. The small company that had had a reputation among its employees for having no advancement opportunities was now a place where opportunity was abundant.

More than just the business had changed. The lives of those involved had also improved. The moms and dads went home and taught The 5C Solution to their children. They showed them how to attain clarity about who they are, who they want to be, and what they want as individuals and as a family. They committed to budgets, vacations, education, and other goals. They prepared to conquer their challenges, created a step-by-step plan and celebrated each step along the way. This simple tool changed the climate of the business by improving morale; improving the lives of those who worked there; and creating loyalty because the team was so grateful for the help and coaching they received.

Businesses are made of people. People have personal problems that they often don't know how to fix or who to go to for assistance that works. They also don't usually have time or discretionary income to spend on personal coaching. By bringing The 5C Solution into the business, they get the answers they need to come to work more focused. This is a unique twist on the problem of low productivity. The usual answer is to give people more skill training, but no amount of training will help if people are distracted with problems at home. People go through relationship problems, children get ill, elder care is needed, they experience financial woes, grieve, and go through all kinds of stress. These are the problems they need help solving.

Once the 5C formula is being used in your company, check in every six months to keep the team and the plans up to date, energized, and moving forward. The 5C Solution creates happy and directed employees, families, and societies.

CHAPTER 8

The 5C Solution in Relationships

Life is complicated. People are complicated. That said, how do we make communication better and create happier relationships? How do we find the fulfillment and love that we crave? How do we keep our relationships solid?

Our most trying circumstances often involve our closest relationships. In fact, the closeness of a relationship can bring out the worst in our communication skills and lead to more serious problems. According to the US Department of Justice, the single largest category of police calls is for domestic violence. Patterns of communication are passed down from generation to generation because we grow up thinking our upbringing was normal. This chapter will show you how The 5C Solution can bring respect and love back into your closest relationships.

The 5C Solution can help with relationships of all kinds. Let's consider five different types of relationships: family, committed relationships, children, friends, and co-workers.

Family

"You can choose your friends but not your family" is an old saying. We may often find ourselves wondering how we are related to these people. There is conflict in all families at one time or another. We are all individuals even though we share the same blood line. We think differently, want different things, have different expectations, and think we know better than those around us. Knowing that, there is bound to be conflict.

There are many different kinds of families today. The unique complications of a blended family will be considered in a later chapter. In this chapter we will discuss people who are related by bloodline or adoption with common parents.

Talk to anyone with a family, and you will find that families that don't have some trouble between siblings, extended family, or generations is a rarity. How do you solve deep-seated differences within a family? Let's use The 5C Solution to work through this.

CLARITY

Consider a problem you are dealing with now with a family member. Ask yourself the following questions:

- ☞ What is the root of this problem?
- ☞ Do I understand the thought process of the other person?
- ☞ What are my expectations in this situation?
- ☞ What am I trying to communicate?
- ☞ What do I want the outcome to be?

COMMITMENT

Make up your mind that no matter what the problem is, you will show respect and act like the person you want to be. Tell someone outside the family of this commitment so they can remind you and help you prepare for tense situations.

CHALLENGES

There are external challenges, such as gossip and hearsay, that create loyalties among different members of a family. When a disagreement occurs, both parties can involve other family members with their side of the story.

Internal challenges exist due to deep-seated emotions going back to when each person was a child. Some feel they weren't treated like their siblings. Their Mr. Prickly can remind them that they didn't feel loved or good enough, which leads to resentment. Identifying the cause of division between family members can be a challenge but is necessary to create a plan to heal division. Ask yourself whether what you are feeling is due to the present circumstances or unresolved childhood resentments.

CREATION OF A PLAN

Communication is the key to creating understanding and unification in families. Putting yourself in the shoes of the other person will go a long way toward helping you understand their point of view. If the other person is abusive or uncooperative, decide what the best way is to deal with this person to maintain your physical health and emotional well-being. There is nothing you can do to change that person, so concentrate on remaining the person you want to be when you have to be in their presence. In other words, create a plan of how you will stay calm, act with respect, and communicate with a loving tone. You can practice responses to words or actions that would normally trigger you into arguments or hurtful comments.

CELEBRATE!

When you honor your feelings and conduct yourself in a respectful manner, even when it is difficult, make sure to celebrate!

Teach The 5C Solution to your family members so you can use it as a basis for communication. It is a game changer for family unity.

Committed Relationships

Whether you are dating, married, or living together, there will be times when you don't see eye to eye with your significant other. The 5C Solution can serve as a formula to gain clarity and avoid serious issues.

You can use the 5C's to tell each other how you feel by starting a difficult conversation with, "I have gotten clarity that I feel _____. I've committed to staying calm and discussing this with you. My challenges are _____. Can you help me create a plan to figure this out?" Be sure to celebrate after you have reached a mutual conclusion.

This may sound simplistic, but it truly works. No one teaches us how to control our emotions, so having the simple formula of the 5C's, and using your fingers to remember it, gives you a tool to use as a guide in emotional moments.

Consider how the 5C's work in the following example:

Paul, a young man in his early thirties, came to see me. Paul and his wife had been fighting recently because she was pushing him to have a baby. Her biological clock was ticking, and she was pressuring him to have sex while she was ovulating. He said he felt like sex was a chore, and there was no romance. He began to avoid her; she would get angry, and they would fight. This had been happening month after month whenever she was ovulating. Additionally, her father was pressuring my client to take over the family business so he could retire with peace of mind. Paul felt like he was living other people's lives and was resentful. He wanted to know how to get them to back off.

We started by having Paul run through The 5C Solution for himself. As he gained clarity on what *he* wanted, he began to realize that he loved working in the family business; in fact, implementing ideas to grow the business excited him. He was able to change his perspective and see that his father-in-law was complimenting him by asking him to take over the business. Being the boss would raise his self-esteem and provide security for his future family. Once his outlook changed, we addressed getting clear about what he wanted for his future.

He wanted to have at least two children, save money to purchase a home for his family, and travel when the children were a little older. I asked him how old he wanted to be when he became a father. He said, "I think I'm ready now." I then asked, "So, you want children as much as your wife does? You're both on the same page?" He smiled and nodded his head. He said, "I've been so busy resisting because I felt like I was being forced, but I really *want* to start a family now!" He laughed at himself.

We spoke about how he could express his commitment to his wife, what challenges they may face moving forward, and how to conquer those challenges. Paul created a step-by-step plan for his future and decided to celebrate each step.

This example shows that the problem can lie with ourselves and with our outlook, attitude, or expectations when we are not clear on what we really want. When we feel pressured by someone else, we can fight against our own true desires. This is due to feeling out of control. Once you discover what you want, you have the control to express it.

Consider how the 5C's work in the following example:

A couple, Tom and Diane, made an appointment with me. Tom told me that Diane had had an affair that was now destroying the marriage. However, when Diane told her side of the story (and there are always two sides), she listed being on the receiving end of verbal, physical, and emotional abuse. She noted Tom had also had several affairs. He also had addiction issues, and she felt trapped in a hurricane of hurt and pain. Diane was a stay-at-home mom with no income, and Tom threatened to take the kids if she left. Emotionally, she had left ten years before. Her affair was a payback for everything he had done to her. They were fighting violently, to the point of police involvement. He wanted to know if the marriage could be saved. She wanted to know how to escape.

Through clarity work, Diane discovered deep-seated emotional pain over the loss of her father, which led her to be attracted to Tom in the first place. Tom discovered that losing his parents at a young age created a void of never feeling loved enough, which led to the affairs and addictions.

Both were raised in volatile households where fighting and emotional abuse was the norm. Putting two broken souls together does not make a whole, solid relationship; it makes a mess. Most of their turmoil had nothing to do with each other. Once they both obtained clarity, they discovered they needed to commit to overcoming their personal challenges by healing themselves separately before they could make decisions concerning their future. They both did the 5C work, and a few months later were able to forgive each other and plan their future together.

The key to this happy result was personal work and learning to communicate with each other about their deepest emotions and needs. They learned empathy for each other and reflected that in their tone of communication.

We have all been in a store and overheard couples snapping at each other, or their children in a sharp, disgusting tone of voice. When a stranger walks by, they immediately change their tone and wish that person a nice day. This shows that they choose to speak to the people closest to them, the most important people in their lives, in ways they would never address a total stranger.

Why do people do this? Sometimes it is habit or the way they were raised. When I was growing up, my mother had a wicked temper. When she was unhappy, everyone knew it. She would yell, slam kitchen cabinet doors, and throw things. My dad was the voice of reason and would say, "That's just your mother." Subconsciously, I grew up thinking this behavior was okay. When I married my first husband and we would have a disagreement, I would yell, slam doors, and throw things. Was that the right way to handle a conflict? No, but I had not learned any other coping skills to deal with my feelings.

After I was divorced and met my new husband, he solemnly sat me down after our first argument and explained that my behavior was not right, and he would not tolerate it. He quietly said, "We can sit and talk like adults." Wow. Okay. This was different! We could have two different opinions, talk about it, and even agree to disagree without verbal assaults or the emotional meltdowns that I was used to.

I can't say my tendency to fly off the handle doesn't rear its ugly head now and again, but I had to commit to changing my automatic trigger when I felt myself getting upset. Truthfully, I didn't like who I was in those moments. I felt out of control and didn't want to be like my mother in how I dealt with conflict. I actually felt more alone and disappointed in myself.

Reacting calmly when you are hurt or angry is hard to do. If you see this tendency in yourself, go back to clarity and figure out why you act or react the way you do. Ask yourself if you like yourself and are being true to the person you want to be when you speak or act in this manner. Commit to speaking to your significant other in the same tone of voice as you do with a friend or workmate. You will be amazed at the difference it makes. After all, we all want to be loved and feel like we matter. By changing this one thing—your tone—you can feel the love you crave and bring peace to your relationship.

Children

Kids as young as five years old have learned The 5C Solution. They love it because it is easy to remember on their hand, and they understand how easy it is to use. In fact, it is often easier for them to gain clarity in what they want and what they feel than it is for adults. Adults tend to complicate what they want by overthinking.

When my younger son was three, he came in the kitchen, looked up at me with his finger on his chin, and said, "I want a . . . banana. Do you have a banana?" I said, "I'm sorry. No. I don't have any bananas. I have an apple, and an orange, and grapes." He hesitated for a moment, said, "No, I just wanted a banana," and walked away. I was stunned because I realized that he had clarity in exactly what he wanted.

This struck me because my older son would just cry when he was that age, and I had to guess what he wanted. I'd say, "Do you want something to eat? Are you tired? Thirsty? Hurt? Why are you crying?" He would just keep crying and scream, "*I don't know what I want!*"

I have to admit that I was more like my older son. It was hard for me to zero in on exactly what I wanted because I was always putting others first. I didn't have opinions. I didn't take the time to get to know what I believed, what I thought, or what I needed. I just went along with what other people said, wanted, or told me to do. I wish I had had The 5C Solution to gain clarity earlier in my own life and my children's as they navigated all the complications of life.

When we have children, life is a whirlwind of activity. Some days seem like they will never end, but then we look back over the years and see how time flew by as the children became adults. I didn't teach them a lot of the basics, like how to food shop, balance a checkbook, invest their money, and make home repairs. I didn't explore different belief systems, professions, or cultures. I didn't have conversations with them about world affairs or expose them to differing points of view. I thought I *had* done these things, but in hindsight, I was just treading water as they grew, due to my own circumstances of living secretly with an alcoholic spouse and just trying to survive. Fortunately, both of my sons are wonderful adults now, but I do wish I had realized these things earlier.

If you have growing children, step back and get your own clarity of who you are, so that you can be an example of what a confident adult looks like. They need to see what love is and how to treat others with respect, courage, and dignity. Have deep conversations with them as you explore every side of subjects. Don't program them to do as you say and not as you do. Commit to giving them the best education about life that you can. Teach them to overcome challenges, especially the ones living inside them. Help them create a plan for their future, and always, always, celebrate them for just who they are. Each child is a unique individual who will never be duplicated. They aren't you. Help them find out who they are, and accept them for just that. Talk to them with kindness, respect, and love. If you start to get agitated, *you* take a time out to gain clarity, commit to being calm, overcome your challenge to fly off the handle, create an environment of unity, and celebrate another day of being a family.

Friends and Co-Workers

Motivational speaker Jim Rohn famously said that we are the average of the five people we spend the most time with. Besides your significant other or family, your friends and co-workers can have a significant effect on who you are. If you don't have clarity in your beliefs, you can be easily influenced by those around you.

The same principles we discussed in using The 5C Solution in other types of relationships apply to our friends and co-workers. If you don't have a clear foundation of proper behavior, beliefs, and what you believe is right and wrong, some of these close relationships can become "frenemies." A frenemy is someone with whom you are friendly despite fundamental differences.

If you are going against your core beliefs or desires when you are with this type of person, you need to gain clarity about why you are with them. It takes strength to say no to an invitation to go out drinking with your co-workers if you would rather not. But if you have a sick feeling in your stomach after you are asked to join them, your body is telling you that you aren't comfortable hanging out. Mixing business with pleasure has its risks. Be mindful of what benefits you.

It takes guts to tell a friend that you disagree with their condescending language or bullying. It isn't only kids who get in bad situations by being in the company of a so-called friend who is a bad influence. There are a lot of people in prison right now because they went along with the wrong group of "friends" and were at the wrong place at the wrong time.

On the other hand, if you have chosen your friends wisely and have surrounded yourself with people who add to your life, then few problems will arise. If differences do arise, you can use the 5C's to communicate clearly and calmly what is troubling you, and then create a plan to overcome it.

Gain clarity on who you want to spend time with. Spending time with friends who add love, support, and fun to your life should be a priority. Commit to cultivating these relationships. Overcome the challenge of being too busy. Create a plan to be with your friends regularly, and then celebrate by laughing with them!

CHAPTER 9

The 5C Solution after a Breakup or Loss

No matter what age you are, if you have had your heart broken, you understand how devastating it feels. After a relationship ends, even if it was mutually agreed on, there is often residual emotions that throw Mr. Prickly into high gear. Doubts about your own lovability can surface.

Loneliness can be all-consuming, resulting in your questioning how you can either get back together or find someone else to fill the void. This is why so many people who leave abusive relationships fall right back into another one. The pain of being rejected or alone is greater than the abuse they endure, and they don't understand that these feelings are part of the grieving process.

How do you gain clarity when you are grieving a recent loss? The 5C Solution can help bring clarity to an unknown future and process the grief that is standing in the way.

Consider the 5C's at work in the following example:

Kim came for coaching after her ten-year relationship with her girlfriend came to a sudden end. It had been extremely difficult for her to come out as gay to her family, which she did after she met Maria. She didn't see this break-up coming. She needed clarity about what had happened, but Maria wouldn't explain. This left Kim feeling bewildered, angry, and depressed.

How do you find closure when you don't understand what happened to a relationship? I worked with Kim to gain clarity of who she is, who she wants to be, and what she wants. During this process, Kim realized that her values were different from Maria's. They had different core beliefs and hadn't really enjoyed each other for some time.

She committed to discovering why they had stayed together as long as they did, when clearly neither one of them was truly happy. The answers were in her challenges. Kim had deep-seated inner thoughts of abandonment because her father had left when she was a small child. She had unconsciously vowed never to leave someone she loved. This led her to avoid admitting how unhappy she was and to blame Maria for all the hurt.

After this revelation, Kim was able to create a plan for her future and the type of relationship she wanted going forward so that she could celebrate her life again.

Grief is often a large part of our lives when we feel lost and confused. My clients often come to me thinking their immediate problem is what is making them feel tired, emotional, and sad. As we begin with the clarity work, they soon realize that an uncommunicated loss in their past is to blame. As we travel through life we experience many losses, such as losing a childhood pet. Our parents tell us not to feel sad, and they quickly replace the pet to try to distract us and turn our normal and natural emotion away from the grief. Unconsciously, this teaches us that acknowledging our feelings of sadness and grief aren't acceptable. Instead, we are supposed to stuff our feelings and either replace the loss or just act happy.

Tears and depression aren't viewed as acceptable social behavior in many parts of the world. At funerals, friends and relatives often have no idea what to say or do to help the grieving. Making things worse, in this age of social media, people simply post, "I'm sorry for your loss" and move on with their lives, feeling as though they have expressed their sympathy and there is not much else they can do to help you. Many times, those with the closest losses are left alone as everyone else returns to their normal routines. Some churches or organizations may arrange for visits, food, or other helpful chores to be done by those who know the family, but that is becoming more and more rare. (In my book *Moving Past the Death of a Loved One*, I explore the feelings of those who are grieving.)

Losses come in many unexpected ways. Moving can mean a loss of friends and familiar surroundings. We can lose trust or faith in someone. The breakup of a friendship or relationship causes loss. Divorce is certainly a loss, and children dealing with parents who are divorcing often feel grief on many levels. They are often confused about why their parents are separating, feel torn between loyalties, are uprooted by being passed back and forth between homes, and feel responsible for the happiness or lack thereof of their parents. In their twenties and thirties, they wonder why they have a difficult time committing to relationships. They may be angry, restless or scared to death of making the same mistakes as their parents. These fears can hold them back from having committed and loving relationships.

We are not taught how to process the emotions of loss, so the feelings get stuffed down into our bodies. The Grief Recovery

Institute has created an effective and beneficial action program for dealing with these emotions. I learned their program to become a Grief Recovery Specialist so I could help those trying to gain clarity and move forward with their lives after loss.

Consider how the 5C's work in the following example:

John, recently retired, was a depressed man who came to me for life coaching. He told me he felt like a failure because he never achieved the level of success he wanted. Since he was mentally still young and not ready to sit in a rocking chair, he came to me to figure out if he could start a consulting business. He said he knew what he wanted to do but could not seem to find the spark to get it off the ground. He couldn't figure out why he had lost his mojo during the past ten years.

As we talked about who he was, his beliefs, and the story of his life, I noted a consistent theme. John spoke of his father and how close they were. All of John's achievements were done to make his dad proud. He smiled and sat up tall as he described their relationship and all of his accomplishments his father had seen. When I asked him when his father had passed away, he said it had been ten years.

A light bulb went off. He realized that when his father passed away, he lost him as an anchor, the one to which he wanted to prove himself. He said he never would have gone to a grief counselor because he hadn't ever connected the dots between his depression and the loss of his father so many years ago.

John gained clarity by completing the Grief Recovery Program so he could communicate and heal the loss. He was then ready to plan his future by finding someone else who would be proud of him, and he chose his granddaughter. He made a commitment that he would report to her about his progress in forming his new business.

We worked on overcoming his challenges, which were the negative voices in his mind telling him he was too old, that it was too late, and that he had missed his opportunity to be the success he had always wanted to be. By creating a business plan, John was able to start his new consulting business, and after each step forward, he celebrated by playing golf, his favorite sport.

Consider how the 5C's work in the following example:

Sarah came to one of my retreats after losing her teenage son, Brett, who was killed in an automobile accident. She said she desperately wanted to move forward but was fixated on his death. She relayed the entire incident in detail. When I asked her when the accident had happened, I was surprised to learn it had been five years earlier; the way she told the story, I thought it was much more recent.

At the time, Sarah was designing an elaborate memorial marker for Brett's grave. She was almost hysterical as she described the details that represented every aspect of his life. She was fearful that people would forget her son, and she wanted strangers who visited the cemetery to know what a gifted young man he had been. She was afraid of leaving out any detail on his memorial marker.

She had been to counselors, clergy, and grief support groups, but nothing had helped. In fact, they made her angrier. Sarah was angry that she was still alive but her son had missed out on life. Her anger heightened during the trial of the person who had caused the accident, as they had taken no personal responsibility. Sarah had been filled with anguish and grief for the last five years, to the point where she said she felt guilty every time she smiled.

After learning The 5C Solution, Sarah got clear that her anger was her way of making sure that Brett was not forgotten. She realized that he wouldn't want her to live a sad and angry life. She committed to doing the grief recovery work so that she could let go of these destructive emotions and let love and joy back into her life. Sarah's challenge was internal. Her Mr. Prickly was feeding her belief that she wouldn't be a good mother if she went on as if nothing had happened. We created a plan to involve her family's support in making future plans that would involve celebrating Brett's life as she took his memory with her into their future.

Sarah also realized that she had been neglecting her other children, their grief, and their ongoing lives during the past five years. While it wasn't fair that her son was missing out on so many opportunities, her other children were missing out on having their mother fully present and happy for them. They were competing for their mother's attention with their deceased sibling, whom they, too, desperately missed. Sarah left the weekend retreat with a beautiful smile and a lightness that she hadn't felt in years due to using The 5C Solution.

Losses and their consequential emotions must be discovered and processed in order to move forward. When you do your clarity work, if you find that you have unresolved feelings as a result of the loss of a loved one, either because they died or because of a divorce or breakup, I highly encourage you to go through the Grief Recovery Institute program. Once you have finished, return to The 5C Solution to plan what to do to move forward.

Please see Resources, page 167, for a link to the Grief Recovery Institute.

CHAPTER 10

The 5C Solution for Teens

Teens deal with a lot of stress. Let's take a look at how The 5C Solution can help them. If you are a parent or loved one reading this, ask your teen to go through the following steps with you. If you are yourself a teen, read this section and answer the questions to help yourself get through whatever issues you are dealing with right now.

When a teenager enters a new middle or high school, their mind can go crazy with thoughts such as, "Will the kids like me? What is this new school going to be like? Will the work be hard? Will I have any friends? Will I get lost in the first few days? Will I forget my locker combination? Will my clothes be cool or made fun of?"

Let's see how applying the 5C's can help as a guide through stressful times.

Applying The 5C Solution

Applying the 5C's to a teenager's issues is no different from using it for other applications. The following is an example of how a teenager can use the The 5C's to address typical teenage feelings and problems when they are starting at a new school.

Clarity: Every other kid is feeling the same thing. No one is smarter, prettier, or better than I am. We are each unique. I will probably get lost, forget my locker combination, and feel weird meeting new kids.

Commitment: I will commit to not taking any of this too seriously. I will confide in (fill in name) to help me when I'm stressed and need to talk.

Challenges: My challenge is my inner voice telling me I'm not good enough or smart enough, and that no one likes me.

Creation of a plan: I will tell my inner voice to stop. Breathe. Ask for help if I get lost. I will laugh at myself and remember that after high school, I probably won't see any of these kids again until we have a class reunion.

Celebrate!: I will celebrate getting through my first day by _____. I will celebrate getting through my first week by_____. I will celebrate my first test by _____.

For Ages Fifteen to Eighteen

Teens in high school often feel the stress of trying to determine the rest of their lives. Their biggest worry is three-fold: which college to attend, which major to pursue, and where to find the money to enroll. In 2014, 62.5 percent of all high school students in the United States went on to attend college. The other 37.5 percent went into a trade or a service position or were unemployed. The pressure to figure out the rest of your life when you are sixteen years old is tremendously stressful.

No one ever figures out their entire life ahead of time. Life changes. Circumstances change and can take us down paths that we may never have imagined. When I was young, I was somewhat of a tomboy. I liked hanging out with my dad and learning how to fix things. I loved building and drawing house plans. When I was in elementary school, I met a friend of my parents who was an architect. We were invited to his house, which he had built. It was the most unique and awesome house I had ever seen. It had started out as a mobile home. Every few years he built an addition onto the home, until it became a multi-level modern work of art. Right then and there I decided I wanted to be an architect.

However, my life took me in another direction because my parents believed that girls did not need an education or career. My second career choice was to be a mom, so I married very young and started a family. I had taken secretarial classes in high school and worked part-time at a law office. I hated that job. I could type 120 words per minute and learned a lot about legal transactions, but I hated being behind a desk all day and not being my own boss.

Twenty years later my path led me back to doing what I loved when I became a home remodeling designer. It was a perfect fit for me, and I realized that what I loved most was designing interior spaces in homes and working with people on the job. It was very close to being the architect I had wanted to be when I was young, but had the added bonus of being more personal and less technical which suited me better.

For many years I sold millions of dollars' worth of home improvements and won many awards. However, after years in that business, my heart sent me in another direction. My commitment to God to help others that I had made in the hospital years before weighed on my heart. Although I had been teaching The 5C Solution as a volunteer at shelters, food banks, schools, clubs, and charitable organizations, I gained clarity that this tool could help a lot more people, so I went from remodeling homes to fixing hearts through my grief counseling and life coaching business.

When I was a teenager, I had no idea that I would be writing books, traveling to speaking engagements, and helping people all over the world find their passions. Although I always enjoyed the ministry work in my former religion, I didn't realize that I would be led to another kind of ministry. This ministry is to help as many people as possible to discover their unique purpose and become the best they can be by learning the 5C's. No one can predict exactly where life will take them, but it will be a journey, and it will be what they make it.

Teenagers need to take responsibility for their own lives. This is part of gaining clarity. Whether they have been raised in a two-parent middle-income household in a small town, or by a single parent who struggles financially in a large city, what matters is what they do with their experience.

Many extremely successful people grew up in foster care in very poor areas. Their experience fueled their determination to become wealthy. On the other hand, there are people who started out in wealthy and famous families who have ended up with addictions, arrests, and severe depression. Teens have a choice. They can either blame their problems on their upbringing or they can set their own course down their own path.

In the following example, the teen's primary stress is figuring out what they want to do after high school. Keeping that in mind, let's see how they might walk through the 5C's:

CLARITY

To gain clarity into the possibilities, I will answer the following questions:

- ☛ What do I love doing?
- ☛ What am I good at?
- ☛ What makes me excited when I talk about it?
- ☛ What were some of the things I liked doing when I was younger?
- ☛ When I was a small child, did I tell people I wanted to be something specific when I grew up? If so, what was it about that career that sounded good to me?
- ☛ What did I spend my time doing when I was younger?

Asking these questions will help narrow down the choices and match careers or opportunities to what this teen likes.

COMMITMENT

I commit to staying true to who I want to be. I will confide in (fill in name), who will understand and guide me through stress and hard times.

CHALLENGES

My inner voice tells me that I'm not good enough, smart enough, strong enough, or popular enough. I am made fun of by other kids who seem to have everything figured out. My parents are pressuring me to figure out what I want to do about college, jobs, and my grades.

CREATION OF A PLAN

Here is my plan to take care of these issues:

- ☛ Remind myself that I don't have to have everything figured out yet.
- ☛ I will spend time getting to know what I like and am good at.
- ☛ I will ask adults about what they do and why, and how they chose their career.
- ☛ I will make a good schedule for studying. I will ask for help in subjects that are difficult for me.
- ☛ I will have a positive attitude. I will laugh at myself when I make a mistake. I will remember that everyone my age feels insecure and that it is a part of growing up.
- ☛ I will have positive, encouraging, authentic people in my space and as my friends.

CELEBRATE!

I will write a list of activities, hobbies, foods, and other things I like. I will refer to this list for ideas to celebrate my accomplishments.

Parents of Teens

One of the most prevalent stresses I see in my coaching practice is kids negotiating their divorced parents. Fifty percent of children in America will be faced with their parents getting divorced. In 2017, the US Census Bureau reported that 32 percent of kids live with a single parent, and only 4 percent of those kids live with a single dad.

It is interesting to note that parents make coaching appointments for their "stressed out, depressed, angry" children, but the kids are often stressed out, depressed, and angry because of their parents, who put them in the middle of their troubled relationship. When a couple splits, it is the child who has to figure out how to love both parents while the parents hate each other.

Tiffany, a fourteen-year-old girl who came to see me, said that she was experiencing headaches, stomachaches, and depression. I asked her when these symptoms would occur. She realized these symptoms only happened when she traveled back and forth between households. Each household had its own vibe, so the anxiety came on whenever she had to change houses. One parent was easygoing, and the other strict.

Tiffany's father had remarried, and he and her stepmother had had more children. Tiffany's stepmother treated her differently from her much-younger half-siblings. She always felt like a babysitter when she came to visit on the weekends, because she was often left to watch her half-siblings so her dad and stepmother could go on date nights. At fourteen, she wasn't equipped to watch a three-year-old and a one-year-old for six hours, especially at bedtime. She had no training and was worried sick that something would happen that she wouldn't know how to handle.

Tiffany was exhausted from school and her own part-time job. She couldn't rest on weekends because she was expected to babysit until the grownups would literally stagger in the door well after one o'clock in the morning. She would stay up most of the night in case the kids woke up, knowing that their parents wouldn't be in any condition to take care of them. By the time she left to go to her other home, it was time to go back to school. Was it any wonder that her grades were suffering? She couldn't tell her mom what was happening at her dad's house because her mom hated her father already.

All of this was kept secret from Tiffany's mom, whom she lived with during the week. Her mom had her own problems. She worked a high-pressure sales job and didn't have time to food shop or cook, so during the week, Tiffany would have to wait for her to arrive home, usually after seven o'clock, with a bag of fast food for dinner.

There wasn't any direct communication between Tiffany's parents, so she was the messenger whenever there were school activities, report cards, medical appointments, travel arrangements, or anything else that needed both parents. Any time there was an activity that she would have loved for both her parents to attend, she would agonize over the anger she would have to endure because each parent would bash the other. Her parents refused to be in the same room together, whether that was at a sports arena with a thousand people, a church with hundreds of others, or a birthday party with close family and friends.

Tiffany loved both her parents. She was not responsible for her parents' damaged relationship, but she was the one suffering the emotional internal battering from negotiating between the two most important adults in her life, and it was sucking the life out of her.

Tiffany's story is not an isolated case. Parents bring their kids to me because the kids are acting out, being rebellious, or are antisocial. They drop them off and hope that I can straighten them out because they "have tried everything." Everything except getting along with their ex-partner. Everything except listening to what is really happening in their kids' lives. Everything except giving them unconditional love and figuring out how not to take out their own stress and frustrations on their kids. When I talk to these stressed out, emotional kids for a few minutes, I know that the ones who should be sitting in the coaching chair are the parents.

It is rare to find divorced or separated parents who know how to fill their children's lives with love and kindness and not put them in the middle of their own chaos. They don't mean to do this, but how often do they bash the other parent to their child when they are angry? How often do they ask personal questions about the other parent so they can know what is going on in their lives? How often do they reinforce that it was the other parent's fault that they aren't a family under one roof anymore? How often do they say they don't have money because of the other parent not living up to their responsibilities?

Children don't tell their parents how much this affects them mentally, emotionally, and physically. They grow up in fear of making one or the other parent angry with them. They walk the tightrope of deciding what to say, do, and tell. It is an added stress on top of school, friends, social media, growing pains, and figuring out who they are.

This generation of kids is nothing like the one just fifty years ago. Their view of relationships has become so jaded that most of them don't want to get married or have kids. If they do have kids, they don't want them to live through the same hardships that they endured. And since they don't have many examples of strong, loving, long-lasting marriages, the chances of them having one is slim. So, we have a generation of young men and women who are disillusioned, troubled, and crying out for acceptance and love. How can The 5C Solution help?

Using the 5C's can bring clarity to what is really happening and what kids can do about it. It gives them a tool to help them make decisions and communicate what they really need. The 5C Solution has mended relationships inside parent-child households and blended families by providing a guide to address the real issues in a calm and logical way.

Let's use Tiffany's story as an example.

CLARITY

Issue: no communication between my parents. I have too much responsibility with babysitting. I am not getting proper nutrition. I feel caught in the middle and want both my parents' support at school functions, parties, and holidays.

What I need: I need training for babysitting and time to rest on weekends. I need my parents to settle issues without my involvement. I want a way to eat healthy food. I want to learn how to communicate my needs.

COMMITMENT

I commit to getting help on how to discuss these issues with my parents. I will learn how to use The 5C Solution in the moment, when emotions are high, to communicate what I really need and to find a solution.

CHALLENGES

My challenges include approaching my parents, fearing retaliation from them, and breaking the current pattern of dysfunction so it doesn't get repeated.

CREATION OF A PLAN

My plan includes practicing clarity. I will ask myself, "What do I need in this moment?" If I could wave a magic wand and solve this problem, what do I want the outcome to be? I know that I can only change my own behavior, so what can I do to get the result I desire?

Regarding the lack of communication between my parents, in a soft tone, I will tell them that I feel torn between the two of them, that I love both of them, and that I don't want to be the middleman during their disputes. I will ask them to attend counseling with me so that the family can discuss how to move forward in greater harmony.

To eat better food, I will ask if I can do shopping online and have food delivered. I can ask someone I know who is a good cook to teach me how to make healthy meals and snacks. I can ask them to FaceTime with me and cook together. I can also watch cooking videos on YouTube. This is a life skill that will serve me well for my entire life. And besides, my parents would be so happy to come home to a home-cooked meal!

I will learn how to speak to my parents as I do to other adults whom I respect and as I want to be spoken to. (Often, our tone of voice and language when speaking to those in our own family is harsh because we allow our emotions to speak for us. We tell them how hurt and angry we are by the tone and words we use, which we would never use with a stranger.) I will give them love, hugs, and laughter. I will remember that they have a lot of stress and responsibility. I will create a new vibe in the house.

Instead of arguing or rebelling, I will be the best person I can be so that I feel good about myself, and then I will radiate that to my family. Will they always recognize it? No, but it is building my character.

I will find adults who can mentor me, people like coaches, teachers, people in my church or neighborhood who are successful. I will ask them for guidance, ride their winds of success, and learn from them. I think they will take me far!

CELEBRATE

I will make a list of things I love to do, and use these as celebrations for when I accomplish anything moving forward. Life is too short not to celebrate!

The information in this chapter may seem simplistic, but the answer to finding and showing love in broken homes is simple when you have a tool that can guide you and remind you what to do in the moment.

Whether you are a parent or a kid, remember to use the 5Cs on your hand and go through each step in the moment when emotions could get rattled.

Little finger, clarity: What do I need in this moment?

Ring finger, commitment: I commit to being calm and communicating my needs and thoughts.

Middle finger, challenges: My emotions take over; my inner voice tells me that this won't work or that no one cares.

Pointer finger, create a plan: Think of one solution.

Thumbs Up, celebrate!: I can celebrate whenever I have a successful communication. I won't always get my way, but if I handle the situation calmly and acknowledge my feelings, I will need to do something to reinforce that success so that I want to do it again. Each time, it will become easier and lead to more happiness in getting what I truly want: love and respect.

CHAPTER 11

The 5C Solution for Blended Families

If you didn't read the previous two chapters on how The 5C Solution helps after a breakup or loss and with teens, I recommend going back and reading them. Even though you may have turned right to this chapter because you are about to tear out your hair trying to find how to get your new significant other to get along with your kids, or your blended family is in chaos, the previous two chapters set the stage for how The 5C Solution will help blend your family and obtain peace and harmony.

Many parents ask me to help their troubled child from their blended or broken family. I call them "broken" families not just because they are no longer living together but because everyone in the family has had their hearts and their "normal" broken. The kids start acting out, and the parents don't know what to do, so they bring them in for coaching. In every single case, these kids, no matter what their age, are grieving the loss of their family unit, angry at having to negotiate divorced parents, and angry at losing the innocence of childhood in the drama from the adults in their lives. The once-married or once-coupled parents don't talk to each other anymore and use their child as the communication conduit. This is a recipe for more hurt, anger, and frustration.

The 5C Solution is a formula that every person in the family can use to gain clarity on their true underlying emotions, to commit to finding their individual peace so they can overcome the challenges of their new living arrangements, create a plan for healthy communication and action, and be able to celebrate with every member of the family.

It is tough enough to experience the loss or breakup of a relationship as an adult, but it is even harder on the kids. They have no say in the decision. All parents should try to shield their kids from the fighting, the hurt, the pain, the cheating, and the real reasons why they end up going their separate ways. However, when they are protected from these things, kids often don't understand what happened to their parents' relationship. If the kids were witness to the breakdown of the relationship between their parents, they become disillusioned and lack respect for one or both of the parents. Let's face it, couples rarely break up with mutual respect and calm negotiations.

Not all blended families are a result of a divorce. If you have lost your spouse to an accident or illness, it is likely that the whole family has never gone for grief counseling. Each person deals differently with such a traumatic experience, and while some individuals are devastated and some appear fine, none of them are taught how to process these emotions. Is it any wonder when anger, bad behavior, or rudeness appears, either from the kids or a new love interest, when a new couple is forming a new family arrangement?

I have been on both sides of this situation. When I found out my mother had started dating a man shortly after my father passed away, I was shocked. To be honest, it wasn't "shortly." It had been two years since I had watched my dad slowly die from lung cancer, but to me, it seemed too soon. After all, my parents had been married almost forty years. I was grown and had a child of my own, but I will never forget walking into the house where I grew up and seeing a stranger sitting in my dad's seat at the dining room table. His back was toward me as I opened the door, and I saw what looked like my dad sitting there reading the newspaper. He wore a red flannel shirt and had short gray hair, just like my dad. I almost screamed because the resemblance to my father was just too close for comfort.

In that moment, I was not thirty-six years old. I was nine, and I wanted to literally kick him out of that chair. How dare he? How dare my mother bring this stranger, who looked like my dad, into the house and let him sit there as if nothing was wrong? I was angry. I was hurt. I was sad.

Logically, I knew this was good for my mother; she had been lost without my father. But now she seemed happier than I had ever seen her in my entire life. That didn't seem fair, either. The way they were acting, it was apparent that they had been seeing each other for a while without telling us. She wasn't apologetic or empathetic to my feelings of shock or sadness. Instead, she glowed as she introduced her new boyfriend. Talk about a whirlwind of emotions!

After the initial shock, I got to know this new fellow. He was nice, kind, and romantic. He made my mom happy. They were traveling, having fun, and making new friends. It was good to know that she had someone to share her life with, but I was still unhappy that my dad wasn't there and that she seemed happier and more affectionate toward this man than she ever was with my dad.

When they got married, I stood by her side with my sisters. The wedding was beautiful—weird for us, but beautiful. I barely talked to her new husband. Every time I saw them together, I felt like a lost, orphaned kid. I was feeling my own unprocessed grief, my own heartbreak of missing my dad. It had nothing to do with my new stepfather.

A little more than a decade later, I faced this scenario from the opposite side. I was now divorced and dating a man with a young son who hated the idea of someone getting in the way of his parents reuniting. They had been divorced for years and were separated for a long time prior to that, but that didn't mean the son was ready to accept that his parents would never reconcile. Although I tried everything I could to be understanding, kind, and patient, it was very hard to be ignored, called Cruella De Vil, and essentially compete with a child for his father's attention. Being a stepmother was not going to be easy.

Blended families come with trainloads of emotional baggage. It doesn't matter what age the family members are. Since fifty percent of marriages in the United States end in divorce, there are a lot of people trying to create new families from broken ones. Let's look at how The 5C Solution can bring peace and harmony to such a family.

The first step, of course, is clarity. How is each person feeling, and why? It doesn't matter if these feelings are logical—which they probably aren't—because there are no right or wrong feelings. Feelings just are.

A few months ago, a man named Andrew called me for help with his blended family. He said he owned a business and was having trouble concentrating at work. However, he was staying at work longer because he hated going home to the tension, arguments, and bitterness that had become everyday life in the home. I could hear the desperation in his voice. He was panicked to think that he could be facing another divorce if things didn't get better, and the last thing he wanted to do was to take sides between his new wife, Suzanne, and his children. Also, his new stepson blamed Andrew's children for the depression his mom was feeling as a result of not being accepted into her new home. The situation seemed complicated and hopeless.

When Andrew and Suzanne came in for their first appointment, they were both in tears. Apparently, there was one adult child, Cheryl, who was stirring the pot of all the anxiety. The ripple effects were creating division between every member of the family, including the parents. Suzanne was in fear of losing Andrew, as he felt he needed to stick up for his children. She was emotionally devastated and felt rejected even though she was trying to be thoughtful and nice. Things had gotten so bad they couldn't even eat dinner at the same table, and Suzanne spent most of her time at home in her bedroom by herself.

As their coach, it was my job to help them gain clarity on what the source of the problem was. On the surface, it looked like Cheryl was just being rude and rejecting her new stepmother. It also looked like Suzanne was taking things too personally, and Andrew was trying to console both sides.

The problems are never what they seem on the surface; those obvious problems are just the tip of the iceberg. The underlying issue with Cheryl was she had never healed the pain of her mother's leaving the family. Her mother had fallen in love with another man and left her father to be with him, but of course she didn't just leave Cheryl's father; she left her children, as well. This kind of rejection can undermine a child's self-esteem. After all, if the one person in the whole world who is supposed to love you unconditionally can leave you, what does that say about your worth?

Just like my ill feelings toward my new stepfather had nothing to do with who he was, Cheryl's animosity toward her new stepmother had nothing to do with their relationship. Cheryl was grieving the loss of her mom, her family as a unit, and the pain of feeling abandoned. She also had cut off communication with her mother due to her hurt and anger at her mother's choices.

Each family member had their own emotions to deal with, but didn't understand anyone else's or how to fix the problems. They needed The 5C Solution.

Once the underlying emotions were discovered through the clarity process, each person could see how the stress was affecting them and the harmful actions they were taking to deal with the stress. Now they could shift from blaming each other to solving the issues together.

Andrew and Suzanne were able to strengthen their personal bond once they realized that they didn't need to take sides. They gained clarity on their strong love and commitment to each other and created a plan to show Cheryl more patience and understanding. Cheryl did grief work to gain clarity on how she felt about her mother and the type of relationship she wanted with her going forward. She was able to reestablish communication and discuss her feelings with her mom. Each sibling learned how to communicate their feelings in a positive and productive way, and the family moved forward in peace and harmony.

This quote from Andrew sums up what they experienced: "We have found Cindy's approach [The 5C Solution] unique compared to others we have tried. She is more direct, yet at the same time honest and compassionate. She was able to get to the root of the issues that threatened the health of our newly blended family, and put us on a better path in only a few short sessions. What could have been months with a typical approach, she did in weeks. She has been through the struggles of blending families herself, so she speaks from a position of experience and is willing to share her personal struggles. We know this contributed to the success of our therapy." This is just one example of how using The 5C Solution can turn a family from the brink of disaster to a success in a short amount of time.

If you or someone you know is having a difficult time navigating their blended or broken family, please know, or let them know, there is help available. Please see Resources page 167 for the link to my YouTube channel.

CHAPTER 12

The 5C Solution for Planning Your Future

How dull life would be if we were born with a manual outlining every experience we will face in our lives. Yes, there are times when we wish we had more insight into our future, and had we known in the past what we know now, we probably would have made different, and hopefully better, decisions. But maybe not. We all do the best we can at the time.

The 5C Solution is a tool that will guide you into your future, and using the 5C's process will lead you down the path toward your ultimate happiness. You have learned that the only way to move toward that goal is to do the clarity work of knowing who you are, who you want to be, and what you want. If you haven't taken the time to do the exercises in this book, please go back and write down your answers on the worksheets.

You are a unique individual. It doesn't matter if anyone else shares your unique belief system. You don't have to convince others that you are right, and you don't have to change to satisfy anyone else.

My mother used to tell me that I looked at life through rose-colored glasses. She meant it as a criticism, that I couldn't see the negative side of things, but I took it as a compliment. She also said, "The world doesn't revolve around you!" But I disagree. *My* world does revolve around me, and *your* world revolves around *you. Your* eyes are looking out at the world, and *your* memories are focused on *your* perspective. Even if you experience an event with other people, you will all remember it slightly differently. No one can tell you that your version is wrong. It is just *your* recollection. The world would be a much better place if everyone looked through the lens of beauty, acceptance, optimism, and love. It would be more fun if everyone were curious about different viewpoints instead of judging others.

When planning your future, stretch yourself. Don't take the safe route. Take the route that is a little dark and dangerous. Light the way with your unique talent and spirit; otherwise, your talents may forever be untapped.

To visualize your future as you create it, ask yourself the following questions:

- What would you do if you knew you wouldn't fail?
- What would you change if nothing were stopping you?
- What is your wildest, most fantastic dream?
- Where do you want to live?
- Whom do you want to be sharing your days?
- What activities make you happy?
- What brings you peace?
- What makes you laugh out loud?

Get very specific. Create a clarity board with pictures or words that represent your dreams. Post it where you see it every day.

Now fill out your answers to the following questions:

Clarity
My most fantastic dream is _____.

Commitment
I will tell (fill in name) that I am going to make my fantastic dream a reality. Nothing is going to stop me!

Challenges
Here is a list of internal thoughts that (name of your Mr. Prickly) will use to try to stop me:_____

_____

Here is the list of external forces (people, places, things) that will try to block my way:_____

_____

Create a Plan
Here are the steps I will take to reach my goal:

X_____**X**
TODAY   **GOAL**

Celebrate!
I will celebrate after each step accomplished by: _____

Conclusion

You have just completed a remarkable journey of self-discovery. Whatever drew you to pick up this book, my hope is that you feel clearer and more empowered to move forward and create an amazing life for yourself. It's been many years since I stood in that hospital room wondering what my life would look like when I went home. I couldn't have imagined all the amazing opportunities that lay ahead. As I got clarity to know who I was and became who I wanted to be, the more peace and calm I felt. I am forever grateful that I lived to experience watching my sons become men, loving again and creating a new family of treasured friends, traveling around the world and meeting people who would enhance my life in so many ways. Every day that I wake up is a celebration of life. Things aren't always easy. Things still happen that I didn't plan or prepare for, but now I'm armed with a tool to handle whatever life hands me. Now you know this tool, so give yourself a "high-five" and practice using your left hand as a memory tool to handle whatever comes next for you! It's been my honor to share this book with you and I'd love for you to share your story with me at cindy@clearpathbycindy.com.

Please share The 5C's with your family, friends and workmates. If you have any questions, or would like to have a personal conversation, follow Clear Path by Cindy on Facebook or Instagram or contact me via my website www.The5CSolution. com. Also, if this book resonated with you, please consider writing a review on Amazon.

Acknowledgements

First and most importantly, I want to acknowledge you the reader. You are the fuel that has kept me determined to share The 5C Solution. It is my greatest hope that what you discover in the pages of this book will be life-changing and bring you to a whole new level of clarity and celebration wherever you are in your life.

I thank my Dad, Stanley Letson, for the warmth, love, and laughter that he brought into my life. He will always be my example of a truly spiritual person, as he gave from his heart to everyone who was in need without seeking any acknowledgment. I miss you every day. While many others let me down, you never did, Dad.

I am forever grateful for my two sons, Jason and Travis. Being your mom has been the highlight of my life. Your love, support, and belief in me inspired me to keep going even when my lack of technical knowledge made me want to scream. I will never forget your hours of building websites and teaching me how to refresh and reboot. Thank you for always being my cheerleaders, forgiving my errors as a parent, and becoming my friends. To my daughter, Bella, who has been a bright light in our lives and the perfect wife to my son Travis.

I want to express my deepest gratitude to my husband, Jay, who taught me my value. You believed in me, supported my passions, and gave me an example of success to follow. When I found you, I realized my vision board wish to have a companion, lover, and best friend. Thank you for understanding my heart and my desire for this work. Thank you also for helping me put my vision on paper.

Another blessing and joy in my life has been the addition of my third son, Jonathan. Thank you for loving me as a second mom and becoming such a spiritual inspiration.

Among those who have supported me along the way and are near and dear to my heart are Claira Percival, my God-given daughter, Fran Hetherington and Jill Kruse, my best friends, and Jeramiah, my Godson. Jill, your insights for the book were invaluable, and I appreciate your expertise and advice more than I can say. Jeramiah, may these words be a guide as you grow and travel down the path of your life.

A special thank you to Stanley El, who walked me through publishing my first book; Stevan Wolf, who believed in the power of the 5C's from the very beginning; Randi Woerner, my graphic designer extraordinaire; and Cheldin Barlatt Rumer, from *This Is It TV*, who brought my message to the masses. Thank you to everyone who shared in editing: Jill Kruse, Dr. Lem Burnham, Larry Steller, Christine Baio and Carrie Mataraza. Thank you to Christy Collins for the beautiful book cover.

I am blessed to have had many mentors. To James Malinchak, who told me to write this book many years ago; Lisa Nichols, who inspired me to tell my story; Sandra Yancey and the e-Women team, where I met so many friends and colleagues that there are too many to mention; Christine Kloser, who chose my book idea as a winner of her Inspirational Author contest, which pushed me to keep going. To Weldon Long, who taught me the importance of Consistent Choices; and to Mike Mataraza, my first coach and continued friend, who gave me permission to design the life of my dreams.

To Steve Harrison and the team at Bradley Communications for all the instruction, introductions, and fun with his team, including the wonderful book coach Martha Bullen. It was the thrill of a lifetime to spend time with Jack Canfield, co-author of the *Chicken Soup for the Soul* series and author of *The Success Principles*, whose influence has been immeasurable. Thank you, Jack, for continuing to share your wisdom with authors who have a burning desire to get their message onto the page and out into the world.

Finally, I would literally not be here if I hadn't been saved by people who cared, and by God, the true author of *The 5C Solution*. Thank you for your grace.

Resources

- For more information about my practice and The 5C Solution, please visit www.the5cSolution.com.

- For information on building a foundation with The 5C Solution, where I walk you through the steps, please visit www.clearpathbycindy.com.

- For information on my online courses, please visit www.clearpathbycindy.com/online-course.

- For information on helping teens and parents navigate issues, please visit www.clearpathbycindy.com/teen-navigating-parents.

- For more information on the Grief Recovery Institute, please visit www.griefrecoverymethod.com.

- For videos on how to get help, please visit my YouTube channel at Cindy Cipriani, Clear Path by Cindy.

- *Moving Past the Death of a Loved One* is available on Amazon.com.

- For information on how to do a 'mind dump' please visit The5cSolution.com/mind-dump.

About the Author

After living in a pit of despair from an abusive marriage, a subsequent divorce and being cast aside by her family and faith, Cindy Cipriani attempted suicide. Twice. In her survival she found the clarity she needed to turn away from hopelessness and toward a healthy life for her and her children.

Cindy built a new path focused on clarity, commitment, overcoming challenges, creating a plan and celebrating accomplishments both big and small.

In the twenty years since those dark days, Cindy has been paying her experiences and wisdom forward as a valued life coach, certified grief recovery specialist, sought-after retreat facilitator and author of her first book, *Moving Past the Death of a Loved One*.

As the Founder of the Clear Path Institute, LLC., Cindy helps individuals, couples and blended families recover from grief, stress and depression. Her empowering corporate training programs have helped employers and staff better manage their life changes to become more engaged, productive and happy.

In this, her new book, *The 5C Solution*, Cindy walks readers through her trademarked process to help people find the root of their problems, reduce their anxiety, and build a guide to the life they really want. Jack Canfield, renowned co-author of *Chicken Soup for the Soul* series, calls Cindy's 5C Solution process brilliant, as it takes a lot of material and simplifies it into a simple tool.

A successful businesswoman, Cindy continues to be a recognized thought leader in the Philadelphia region. *The Philadelphia Business Journal* recognized her with its South Jersey Entrepreneur Award. *South Jersey Biz Magazine* named her to its 25 Women to Watch list, she has served as Mentor at the Bizwomen Mentoring Monday in Philadelphia and has taught at the Center for People in Transition at Rowan College.

Cindy is a keynote speaker, conference closer and workshop facilitator for business groups and schools, and has served on many nonprofit boards and community initiatives, including as the campaign chairperson for The United Way of Gloucester County. To learn more or to book Cindy to speak, visit www.the5csolution.com.

Additional helpful materials:

To get additional information and tips on how
The 5C Solution can be used in your life and business:

Follow *Clear Path by Cindy* on Facebook & Instagram

Hire Cindy to speak to your organization,
sales team or non-profit.

Order The 5C Solution online course on The5CSolution.com

Contact: hello@clearpathbycindy.com

If you enjoyed this book and want additional help in coping
with grief, order *Moving Past the Death of a Loved One*.

This daily reading book offers insight and useful tips
on self-care and healing of those who are making
their way through a personal loss.

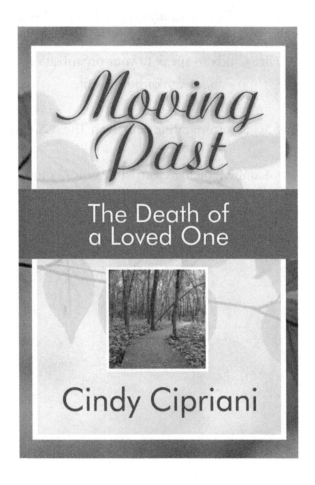

Made in the USA
Middletown, DE
04 January 2021